RELIVING PAST LIVES

RELIVING
PAST LIVES

The Evidence Under Hypnosis

by HELEN WAMBACH, Ph.D.

HARPER & ROW, PUBLISHERS

New York, Hagerstown,

San Francisco, London

TO MY SUBJECTS
who together provided me with the data in
this book and the zest to explore further

FIRST EDITION

Designed by C. Linda Dingler

Library of Congress Cataloging in Publication Data

Wambach, Helen.
    Reliving past lives.
    1. Reincarnation—Case Studies.   2. Hypnotism—Case studies.   I. Title.
BL515.W34   133.9′013   77–11805
ISBN 0–06–014513–7

78 79 80 81 82 10 9 8 7 6 5 4 3 2 1

CONTENTS

FIGURES AND TABLES

FIGURES

TABLES

1

THE START

The year was 1966; the place was Mount Holly, New Jersey. The actor in this particular drama was I. I was a psychologist at Monmouth Medical Center in Long Branch, New Jersey. My life was full of activities, including teaching at the local community college. I had no particular reason to explore my inner feelings, and I had had no mystical feelings in the past that I could recall. I certainly didn't think of myself as "psychic."

These are the thoughts that went through my mind as I slowly came out of a daze. I was standing in a small room filled with musty old books in the upstairs of a Quaker memorial that I had come to explore that day. For the past fifteen minutes I had been in what I now realize was an altered state of consciousness. The book that had impelled this was still in my hand as I reoriented myself to the here-and-now. I glanced down at the book in my hand, but now it had lost its power to transmit me to a previous time and place.

When I first entered the house, I was just a Sunday tourist coming to visit an obscure memorial. As I mounted the stairs to the second floor, a feeling of being in another time and place came over me. As I entered the small library room, I saw myself going automatically to the shelf of books and taking one down. I seemed to "know" that this had been my book, and as I looked at the pages, a scene came before my inner eye. I was riding on a mule across a stubbled field, and this book was propped up on the saddle in front of me. The sun was hot on my back, and my clothes were scratchy. I could feel the horse moving under me while I sat in the saddle, deeply absorbed in reading the book propped before me. The book I was reading was a report of a minister's experience of the between-life state while he was in a coma. I seemed to know the book's contents before I turned the pages.

Only a few moments passed before I returned to the present. This experience was upsetting to me, because I had thought of myself as a conventionally "respectable" psychologist with no obvious signs of mental disturbance. Why had I experienced this disorientation? Why did I feel that this was my book? And, most curious of all to me, why was I suddenly experiencing myself in another body in another time period?

The experience shook me. I had had interesting dreams, and I was aware of all of the theories of subconscious functioning that could explain my own experience. I knew that *"déjà vu"* was the official name for my experience; I had read Freud's monograph on it. Yet I was unprepared for the vividness and immediacy of this experience. I wasn't psychic! I had been moderately interested in J. B. Rhine's work in ESP, but had not been involved in any explorations or research myself. I remembered when the book on Bridey Murphy's hypnotic past-life recall had been published when I was in graduate school. My professors treated it scornfully, and I went along with their judgments. I assumed that rational explanations could be found for all such experiences.

This personal encounter with the mysterious opened me to an awareness that there were many mysteries that had not yet been solved. Was my experience fantasy, or did it reflect a reality I had never suspected before?

It has taken me ten years and more than two thousand hypnotic regression sessions to come up with an answer to that question. As I traced the final line on my graph "Sex Distribution in Past Time Periods," for my second, replication study of 350 cases (my original sample was 850 cases), the answer lay before me, neatly outlined and expressed in the numerical form that I found most persuasive. My subjects divided themselves into 49.4 percent past lives as women and 50.6 percent past lives as men—a biological fact in past time periods. These subjects could not have arrived at this by telepathy, fantasy, or chance alone. Past-life recall did accurately reflect the past.

But as is so often the case, the exploration was the enlightening experience rather than the final result. In this book I will share with you the false starts and frustrations, the surprises, and the gradual insight I developed through the experiences shared with my subjects in this research. I could have written the results in professional journal form, letting the graphs and tables in Chapter 8 represent the reality of my experimentation. But in many ways our "scientific" techniques distort the reality of the human search for new knowledge and understanding. Physicists tell us that "hard reality" is actually a process; that each atom, each molecule, exists not as a separate entity but as part of a dynamic process involving all the other atoms and molecules. This is even more true of human research; myriad interactions, coincidences, the flash of shared insight—all combine to produce the results of any experiment.

As I plunged deeper into the work of hypnotic regression, I was reminded of many therapy cases I had dealt with since 1955, when I first began practicing psychotherapy. I felt a deeper understanding of cases that had puzzled me then.

Linda—a small, frail five-year-old. Ageless brown eyes in a pinched face, eyes full of hostility, apparently reflecting a fierce determination to avoid human contact. Linda couldn't—or wouldn't—talk, or respond to the psychological tests I tried to administer. I took her into the playroom. She pulled away from my hand, took up a book, and crawled under the table. I listened, and heard her read the book softly to herself. Her mother reported that she was able to read, though no one had taught her. From infancy, Linda had avoided human contact. She played only with mechanical objects, or wrote figures on a blackboard. She demonstrated amazing mathematical skill in constructing strange games with numbers on her blackboard, but she would not speak or allow herself to be held or touched by other human beings. A case of infantile autism; the diagnosis was clear. Would therapy help? The literature on autistic children was not encouraging, but I wanted to try.

I spent ten months with Linda in that playroom, one hour a week. And I was witness to a miracle, and participant in that miracle, without ever understanding what was happening. I operated on instinct with Linda. Now I understand that I communicated telepathically with her, although at the time I didn't perceive or formulate it that way. I only knew that I focused intently on her, without trying to invade her space physically. It was three weeks before she gave me a sign. She picked up a toy telephone and spoke to me through that. She wanted to play "baby," but I was to be the baby. For one hour a week over a two-month period, Linda force-fed me water from a baby bottle. She was showing me how much she hated the passivity, the helplessness of infancy. Until she made me experience it, she could not relate to me. Finally, I understood. Though I don't remember how I signaled this to Linda, I found that the game changed. She touched me for the first time. I waited for two more sessions before I dared to touch her. She stood very still, not responding to my hug, but not turning away.

Therapy proceeded quickly after that breakthrough. Linda and I sang nursery songs together, played with finger paints. One day, her hands smeared with brown paint, Linda turned to me and said her first words in communication to another human being. "Oh, happy shit!" she proclaimed. She smeared my hands with paint and examined them carefully, comparing them to her hands. It was as though Linda were discovering her physical body and my physical body. One day, after examining my hands carefully, she looked directly into my eyes and spoke a complete sentence. "I'm Pinocchio and you're the Blue Fairy," she said softly. She had decided to come alive.

Linda moved rapidly through the stages of young childhood, and after ten months she seemed like a normal five-year-old. She was attending kindergarten. She had lost her ability to read and do mathematical calculations, but was learning to write her name along with the other five-year-olds in her class. Linda's family moved away at that point, and I don't know what happened to her. But I feel now that Linda had rejected her body in this lifetime, perhaps because of an unpleasant infancy. She maintained a past adult personality in a child's body, refusing the challenge of growth in a new body and a new personality. Somehow she then made the decision to accept this life. The strange adult talents disappeared and a normal child emerged. Is it possible that childhood autism is a refusal to join a new body?

If the anecdote I have described here indicates that I was a magical, always-effective therapist, be assured that this was not the case. I saw many people who did not change, and several who grew worse. It was as though there were certain patients who were on the same wavelength as I; and I could work well with these. In other cases my efforts didn't seem to result in any true connection, and no improvement took place.

One of the cases in which my therapeutic ability seemed to have no effect at all was Peter, a five-year-old black youngster who was brought for treatment because of hyperactive behavior and an inability to relax or settle down in the classroom. His mother was a small, anxious woman who said she knew of no reason for his disturbance. He had been checked out by the family doctor, and no reason for his inability to concentrate could be discovered in the physical examination, so the doctor referred him for psychotherapy.

Peter spent no longer than ten seconds with each toy in the playroom, running from one to the other as though driven, so I took him to my office. He was too distractible to be able to perform well on the psychological tests, and I wanted to establish a rapport with him before I began testing him. At last, he was willing to sit on my lap and talk. To my complete astonishment, he began talking about his life as a rookie policeman. He talked about how he played basketball, and said he wished he'd be able to smoke. He said he liked smoking cigarettes before and didn't know why he couldn't now. It took me awhile to realize that Peter was talking about a past life. At first, I thought he was relating some story he had seen on television, but the more he spoke about it, the more it seemed he was describing some experience he felt had been his own. I was curious about his policeman experiences, so I encouraged him to talk about them more. This surprised Peter, because he told me that only his three-year-old sister had ever listened to him when he talked about "the policeman."

When I asked Peter's mother whether he had ever discussed this past life with her, she reported that he had begun talking about it when he was about three. "I told him he shouldn't make up stories, and then he didn't talk about it much anymore," she reported.

I worked with Peter in the playroom for three months. His hyperactivity continued, though he was able to sit and relax when he discussed his life as a policeman with me. The subject seemed to obsess him, although this may have been because I was the only person other than his small sister who would listen to him. One day his mother reported that a policeman had brought him home because he was out in the middle of the street trying to direct traffic. I felt slightly guilty, because he had told me about his traffic assignment in his life as a policeman and apparently was beginning to act out his past-life recall—worrisome behavior for a five-year-old.

Peter's behavior showed no signs of improvement. He was withdrawn from treatment, and I have no idea what became of the bright-eyed little boy who remembered his past life.

Since that time, I have felt that it is not wise to encourage young children to recall past-life experiences. It certainly didn't help Peter, and seemed to make his adjustment to this life more difficult. From the perspective of twelve years later and after the observation of many hypnotic regressions into past lives, I still feel that it is wiser for people to recall past-life experiences only when they are mature enough to cope with them. A premature immersion in experiences that may have been traumatic merely adds to the burden of adjustment in our present life. I have heard it said that wisdom is passion remembered in tranquillity. It may be that past-life recall comes to us most usefully when we have mastered the reality of our here-and-now time and our here-and-now life.

Though my experiences with children in therapy moved me closer to understanding the telepathic nature of communication, several adult cases also led to my research into past lives.

John had been referred for treatment because a developing phobia reduced his effectiveness on his job and made it very difficult for him to maintain a normal life. His problem began when he was walking through the woods near his home one day and discovered a dead body. He reported the body to the authorities and they questioned him briefly. He heard nothing further, and for several days his life went on normally. Then he woke one morning in a sweat of apprehension. He tried to maintain his daily routine, which involved driving to work at the local plant, where he had done well and had ten years' seniority. He enjoyed his job, and he didn't know why he was experiencing a terror of leaving his home. At first he forced himself to drive his car to work, but as his fear of being out on the open highway increased, this became impossible. He said he was afraid of someone following him, and finally told me he was afraid the Mafia was out to get him and his wife. He believed that the body he had found was a victim of the Mafia, and the fact that he had reported it to the authorities meant that he was now in trouble with the mob.

His agoraphobia increased. He found it very difficult now to leave the house for any reason, and began missing more and more days on the job. He had been placed on Librium medication for his anxiety, but this had not helped appreciably. Soon he was working only half-time, and this meant hardship for his family. His wife was a sympathetic person and helped him in every way she could, driving him to and from the plant and reassuring him constantly, but nothing seemed to work.

Because of the man's fear that the Mafia was following him, I began to probe into the possibility that this was the beginning of a paranoid psychosis. He showed some of the classic signs of paranoia, including a hyperawareness of what everyone around him was saying and a tendency to misinterpret gestures. He also evidenced a problem common to many schizophrenics, the inability to sleep. He seemed to be afraid of his dreams, and to resist sleeping at all unless he was heavily dosed with barbiturates.

I spent the first month of therapy with John in helping him to become more comfortable with me, and as I talked with him I began to discard the notion that this was a paranoid psychosis. His relationship with others in his family seemed good; he was experiencing no hallucinations, such as voices talking to him; and his fear of the Mafia was based, however slightly, on reality. Mafia executions had taken place in this part of the state, and the fact that nothing was reported subsequently about the body tended to support his notion that the authorities were not pursuing the investigation with much vigor.

John's condition did not improve, and my usual approaches were not working. In desperation, I decided to use hypnosis. I had learned this technique during my internship in a Veterans Administration hospital, where victims of combat fatigue were hypnotized and brought back to the experience in combat that had caused the problem. When they were able to reexperience the trauma and remember it fully, their symptoms often eased. Hypnosis was now out of fashion as a therapy device, however, and I didn't feel very comfortable using it, but it was worth a try.

Because John now trusted me, it was possible to get him to relax. I took him back through his childhood. I knew that he had been raised by an uncle and aunt and remembered nothing of his early childhood years. Perhaps we could find something in this early childhood that would explain the current phobia. I used the usual hypnotic relaxation techniques as he lay back in the chair in my office. I took him back to the age of ten. He responded to my questions as a ten-year-old might. He appeared to be a quiet and somewhat withdrawn boy, but said he had no particular problems. He had a mild affection for his aunt and uncle, but the relationship seemed distant. I moved him further back into his childhood, to the age of five. Now he answered my questions in very simple syllables, but expressed much more emotion than he had at ten. He was an unhappy child. He told me he had bad nightmares, but didn't say much about the content. When I asked him where his mother was, it seemed as though he were about to cry. "I don't know. I want to see my mommy." Then I moved him back to the last time when he had seen his mother. He apparently regressed to a time somewhere between the ages of four and five. He was in a small house in the woods. He was upstairs in the bedroom. "Mommy and Daddy are yelling at each other." I asked if he was scared, and he nodded his head. I probed further. "Oh! Daddy's pushing Mommy." In the unfolding story, he ran downstairs and out the door of the house. It had been snowing, he told me, and in a snow bank outside the bedroom window he found the body of his mother. She was dead. I encouraged him to express the feelings he had at that time, but suggested that when he came out of hypnosis he would be able to view the incident with detachment and it would no longer hold any terrors for him.

When he woke up from the hypnosis, he expressed amazement at what had happened. "I've seen that house in my dreams. I didn't realize that's where I lived when I was small. More and more of it is coming back to me now. I don't think I ever saw my mother or my father after that night. I guess the authorities took me away, and my aunt and uncle came to get me."

He sat silently for a few moments. Then he looked up at me and said, "So that's why I'm so afraid of dead bodies. Maybe that's why I cling so to my wife now. I'm afraid I'll lose her the way I lost my mother."

John decided that he wanted to explore the matter further by writing to his uncle for details. However, he never told me the result of these inquiries, and whether the story that unfolded under hypnosis had actually occurred remains a mystery to me. There is a tendency to assume that witnesses regressed to the scene of a crime will tell the truth under hypnosis—that hypnosis results in perfect recall. But does it? When a particular detail, such as a license number, can be checked, then hypnosis can be assumed to uncover "the truth." But when there is no objective evidence to confirm hypnotic regression, then we must approach the material reported under hypnosis with caution. What I do know is that John improved rapidly. Within two weeks he was able to drive a car by himself and to resume his job full time.

In John I had seen a dramatic instance of hypnotic regression that resulted in marked improvement of a severe phobia. Was it because we had uncovered the trauma that lay beneath the immediate problem? I had no way of documenting the truth of the story that emerged under hypnosis, but it satisfied John, and it enabled him to resume a normal life. And it set me on a possible trail. If remembering childhood traumas could cure phobias, would remembering past lives also cure phobias resistant to other treatment?

It is not only the patients I have seen in therapy who have taught me that the depths of the human mind have not yet been charted. Freud, Jung, Adler, the behaviorist John Watson—all these men offered insights that illuminated only a small corner of the human mind. I learned a great deal about the complexities of human functioning from my students in my college classes.

I was teaching Abnormal Psychology, and as a class assignment, I asked the students to remember at least one dream and bring it to class, so that I could illustrate dream analysis. This resulted in very lively class sessions, and I was pleased at the way my students seemed to be grasping the principles of abnormal psychology through understanding their own dreams. One of the course members, Sheryl, related a dream she had had the previous night. She dreamed that she had been in a car with several of her fellow students, and they were driving very fast. Suddenly, the car came to a curve, missed the curve, and crashed. In the dream she seemed to be standing above the scene of the crash, and with a sense of shock she saw her own body lying by the roadside. Her head had been severed from her body. The feeling in the dream was not so much nightmare as wonderment at being outside of her body.

Sheryl's dream allowed me to illustrate with relish my point that dreams deal with everyday realities. I said that she was probably in conflict about choosing between having fun while she was in college, and the need to study. I told her I thought this severing of her head from her body indicated to her that unless she settled down with her studies, she was likely to have problems when exam time came around. Sheryl laughingly agreed with this, and the class was both amused by and interested in this example of dream analysis. "Well, it looks like I have to hit the books," she said as she left the classroom.

Then I forgot the entire incident. The semester ended shortly after Sheryl related her dream, and I began teaching another course. It was three months later that I encountered one of my former students from the Abnormal Psychology class. "Do you remember the day Sheryl told her dream about the automobile accident?" he asked me. I thought for a few moments, and then the memory of it came back to me. "Yes, I remember it. How's Sheryl doing?" He looked at me solemnly for a moment and I became aware that he was upset. Then he spoke. "Last week Sheryl was in an automobile accident. She was killed. A piece of the auto nearly severed her head." I sat down on a bench in horrified silence. He went on, "A few of us who were in your class last semester remembered Sheryl's dream. What do you think it means? Can we all see our deaths ahead in dreams?" I didn't know what to say. My elaborate analysis of her dream, which seemed so clever at the time, crumbled. Sheryl had foreseen her own death. Shaken, I turned to him and said, "I don't know. I don't know how to look at this thing. I'm shocked by it. But I do remember that Sheryl said it was not a nightmare, so perhaps she knew how she was to die, but that it was all right with her." I got up and hurried on to my next class, trying to put the incident in the back of my mind, because I had no way to deal with its implications. But Sheryl's story is one of the many happenings in my life that led me toward research on dying.

To be an "expert" on the human mind is to be humbled again and again by its mysteries. I think I knew more about psychological theory, and had greater confidence in my own ability to diagnose and treat psychological problems, when I first left graduate school than I have had in the twenty years since then. Again and again I have been awe-struck by the remarkable qualities of the mind; the easy labeling that is so popular in our culture becomes very unsatisfactory when you deal daily with human beings in trouble. What most people casually call "fantasies" or "dreams" became vast uncharted regions that have kept me moving toward a broader understanding of the mind. I don't feel I have achieved any great understanding yet, but twenty years of dealing with people have taught me the wisdom of listening rather than diagnosing, of living with rather than "treating" other people. I have become disillusioned with the patient-therapist relationship as a means of exploring "truth," though I do value the warmth and the quiet openness of the therapy hour. I am most grateful to all the people who presented themselves to me as "patients," and who thereby taught and directed me in ways that I could never have reached on my own.

I wanted to know more. I wanted to apply what I had learned about scientific method to the areas that most people shove aside as being of no importance. I began to realize that I must explore the depths of the mind instead of limiting myself to those superficial exchanges that in our society pass for "knowing" each other. It was time to begin my research.

2

MORE STRANGE
ADVENTURES

The 1960s brought social upheavals, changing life styles, and—
for me—new experiences in psychotherapy. The clinic and the hospital where I worked began seeing young people who had had
bad trips on LSD, and I discovered that the techniques I used
with therapy patients weren't very effective in coping with distur-
bances caused by psychedelic-drug ingestion. I remember working
with one young woman who had taken LSD before our therapy
session. I found myself engrossed in her answers to my questions;
instead of discussing her problems, she described the folds in the
curtains on my office window, the images she was receiving as
she closed her eyes and turned inward, and the feeling she had
that she was, at times, outside of her body.

What was this? The way in which she described her experiences
was different from that of the psychotics I had seen in therapy.
Psychotics often described the voices they were hearing and gave
delusional explanations of the origin of their strange mental happenings, but my LSD subject seemed to be enjoying her disorientation
and the onrushing sensory impressions that came to her while she
was on the drug.

What appeared to be happening with LSD was that areas of
the brain that normally function outside conscious awareness sud-

denly flooded the conscious mind and overruled the organizing ability of the ego to manage and control them. There is some experimental evidence to suggest that LSD and some other psychedelics increase the production of acetylcholine at the nerve synapses, causing the circuitry of the brain to function in a wide-open way. An analogy is a telephone switchboard in which all the circuits are thrown open, so that many simultaneous conversations are heard at the same time. I don't believe the content of the experiences LSD subjects report is affected by the drug. Instead, it is my observation that the drug acts to bring into awareness a vast amount of subconscious or unconscious functioning; and these thoughts, images, and emotions are allowed to penetrate through to the conscious mind.

In a sense, the same process occurs in schizophrenics. However, schizophrenics try to find reasons why their everyday world has taken on new shapes and colors, why dramas are taking place in their mind's eye, and why they see meanings in things that ordinarily have no meaning. The schizophrenic builds up a delusionary system that helps him explain why he is experiencing these phenomena. He may believe he is being persecuted, that others are sending radio messages through his head, that he is the center of the universe, and that all that takes place in the world is directed toward him; or he may believe that he has come from another planet and that is why he sees the world differently from others around him.

We are told that we use only 10 percent of our brain. I have come to believe that those portions of the brain that we think of as having no specific function—the remaining 90 percent—are indeed operating constantly. But the ego—the "everyday self"— serves as a switchboard operator, allowing into consciousness only that which is purposeful and meaningful to the goals and belief of the individual, and to the social reality that he or she shares with others in the culture.

The people who took LSD thought that what they were experiencing was a product of the drug, so they didn't think about *why* they were seeing, feeling, and hearing new things. It was simply what happened when you were on a "trip." When LSD was first traded on street corners, there were many cases of young people reporting to hospitals in panic. Once the youthful counterculture became aware of what LSD trips could be like, the admissions to hospitals dropped. At first we thought this was because there were fewer psychedelic drugs around, but it soon became evident that was not true. What apparently happened is that one drug user told another what to expect, and explained that the experience would be over within twelve hours. Once the ego knew this, it could relax and allow the LSD experiences to flow through because it now had a label for them. This was not insanity; it was a psychedelic "trip."

As I saw these young people in both my clinic office and in private practice, I grew more and more intrigued by their experiences while under the drug. Several of them told me about flashes of past lives they glimpsed after taking it. This struck a chord in me because of my recent *déjà vu* experience in the Quaker memorial. The psychedelic experience seemed to open the young people to awarenesses that their own culture had not prepared them for. I noticed that some began to read the literature of Eastern mysticism, and found in it a few answers that connected with their experiences with the drug.

I questioned the young people cautiously about their ESP experiences and their *déjà vu* experiences with drugs. I explained to them that they could explore the same phenomena under hypnosis, which offered more safeguards and fewer hazards than drugs. It was also both free and legal. I soon found that most of the young people went into hypnosis easily. For a time, I thought that people who had taken LSD were by definition good hypnotic subjects, but I have since learned that this is not the case. In part, the reason I had so many successful hypnosis trips with the LSD young people was simply because they were young. The younger the subject, the easier it is to induce hypnosis.

One of my first subjects for systematic hypnotic regression to a past life was Mark. Mark, who had had psychedelic experiences, enjoyed his job, was well adjusted socially, and was not using LSD at this time. During a visit to Europe the previous year, he was driving through northern Italy and came to a bend in the road. It seemed oddly familiar, and the sense of *déjà vu* grew as he drove up a hill and saw a small stone building lying to his right.

"I knew I had seen that building before. A feeling came over me almost of sadness. I seemed to know the place, and the place had real meaning for me. Yet at the same time I knew it wasn't happy," he told me.

Mark volunteered for the hypnotic trip because he wanted to know more about this experience. He proved to be an excellent hypnotic subject, and reached a fairly deep stage of hypnosis after three minutes of induction. He was initially regressed to his tenth birthday, and reported vividly the pictures that came to his mind. He recalled the names of his friends who were at the birthday party, a sign to me that he was indeed under hypnosis. Small details, such as names of childhood companions, are difficult to recall when we are in the conscious waking state, but they emerge quite clearly under hypnosis.

From his tenth birthday, Mark was taken back to the more distant past. I told him, "You are now going back in time. Your mind will be alert and you will be able to report what you see." Mark was then told that it was the year 1900. "Tell me what you see," I instructed him.

"I . . . don't know. Faces slipping by me. It's all hazy." There was a long pause as Mark stirred restlessly in the chair. I deepened the hypnotic trance, and once again took him back in time.

"We are going back in time again. It is now 1870. Tell me what you see."

Mark's eyelids flickered, and it was apparent to me that he was seeing images. I find that this rapid eye movement, which is characteristic of the dream state, is also present under hypnosis when the subject is visualizing.

"It's . . . I see the street and the buildings. I see the street, there are cobblestones, it's rough. There are uniforms around me."

I also knew from my informal sessions with students that I could get subjects "into" a past lifetime by asking them to look down at their bodies and describe what they were wearing. I asked Mark to look down at his feet.

"Boots. I am wearing something like a uniform too. It's white and blue. The people around me are running. There seems to be some kind of confusion or battle."

"What is your name?" I asked.

Mark seemed to be struggling. "I don't know, can't think of it. But there's a friend next to me. I think he is Pierre."

I tried a technique I had found to be useful in getting people to recall their names. "Pierre turns to you and says something to you. He uses your name. What does he call you?"

"Paul. That's my name, Paul."

All I had now was the information that he was dressed in a blue-and-white uniform, was standing in a cobblestone street with other uniformed soldiers, and that there was a lot of confusion around. I needed to know more in order to identify this event and the time period. I asked Mark, "Do you know where you are? What is happening?

"I think . . . I think it's Paris." Mark still seemed to be seeing pictures, because his eyelids were moving. An expression of discomfort crossed his face, and he was silent for a long time. It was my impression that whatever he was experiencing was unpleasant for him, so I decided to move him ahead and out of that episode. "You will now move ahead in that lifetime to the day that you die. You will tell me what happens without experiencing any pain or any fear," I told him.

When Mark spoke in answer to my question, his voice was very low. I find that when hypnotized subjects are in the very deepest state, it is difficult for them to be able to articulate clearly, and their voices are almost inaudible.

"I'm in some sort of big tent or building. I can't see very well, I'm wounded. There are a lot of other men around me. I hear their cries."

Once again I assured Mark that he would feel no pain or discomfort, and would stay detached enough to be able to tell me what happened. I asked him if he was frightened, and Mark replied, "I think I am going to die. It's a big room, there is some kind of doctor here. Oh!"

Mark moved restlessly in the chair and I felt that he was experiencing pain in spite of my instructions. I quickly moved him out of the scene and relaxed him once more. I told him that his mind would remain alert, but that he would feel neither sorrow nor pain. "Now you are dead. Can you see what they are doing with your body?"

"It's . . . it's kind of hazy. My body seems to be piled up with a lot of other bodies. I don't know. . . ." and his voice trailed off into silence.

This was extremely interesting. Mark had had no idea of having led a life in the 1800s, and certainly not in Paris. What we were looking for was the *déjà vu* experience in Italy. I decided to move him still further back in time to see if we could uncover the Italian episode. I told him, "Now you are drifting peacefully along. You feel very easy and relaxed. You are floating backward through time. It is the year 1600. Do you see anything?"

Mark stirred a little in the chair. His eyelids flickered slightly and he said, "Just faces drifting along. No, don't really see anything, just misty haze."

"We are going back through time again. It is the year 1450. Do you see anything?"

Mark's eyelids began to flicker rapidly. He responded after a moment by saying, "A hill. I'm riding and I see the hills and the trees."

I asked him to look down at his feet and at the lower part of his body and tell what he was wearing.

"It seems to be . . . oh, I'm wearing some kind of metal. I guess it's a suit of armor, but it doesn't seem very heavy."

"What do you see around you?" I asked Mark.

"I'm coming up to a large fort or building. I guess it's a castle . . . it's my castle . . . it isn't really very big."

"How old are you now?" I asked.

"Don't know. I'm a man . . . don't know how old."

"Do you know what your name is?"

There was a long silence; once again I ran into the difficulty of finding the name in the past life. I moved on to the next question. "Are there any people around you?"

"I have my men with me. We're going into the castle."

"One of the men calls you by your name. What does he call you?"

"I think it's . . . Graf something."

I was surprised at the title and curious about his companions. "These men, do they work with you?" I asked him.

"We are fighting. They fight with me."

"Who are you fighting for?"

"The Holy Roman Emperor."

"Is your family in the castle?"

"No." There was a pause here, during which Mark seemed to be experiencing some strong emotions. He continued by saying, "I don't have any family. I don't have a wife."

I decided to explore this further, because it was apparently the Italian lifetime about which Mark had had the *déjà vu* experience on his trip to Italy the previous year. I didn't know Mark's age in 1450. I wanted to know more about his childhood in that lifetime, so I moved him back further in time. "It is the year 1435. Go back to 1435. Tell me what you see."

"A large courtyard. I'm working on a horse. Taking care of a horse." Mark seemed to be responding more quickly to my instructions, and his eyelids were moving rapidly. I asked him, "Is it your castle?"

"No. It's very big. I seem to be—well, I work with the horses. There are lots of people around. I like it here."

Apparently, Mark was not with his family but was serving as a page or attendant in a larger castle. If it was 1435, and he was in his mid-twenties or early thirties in 1450, I would be tapping into his memories at age ten to fifteen in the Italian lifetime. I was curious as to how he had come to the castle and about his job with the horses. "When did you arrive at this castle?" I asked him.

"Been here a long time. I want to be a knight like the others when I get old enough." Mark described activities that seemed to be largely grooming and feeding horses and listening to the older men talk.

I was curious about the death experiences in this lifetime, because Mark had told me he felt sadness when he saw the small stone castle on his trip to Italy. What was the reason for this sadness? Did it connect with his death in that life? I asked him, "You are now going to move ahead in time to the day that you died in that life. You will remember everything that happened, but you will feel no pain. You will remain relaxed and somewhat distant, even though you will reexperience everything you felt then." I checked Mark's state of hypnosis by lifting his arm. He did not waken or stir as I tested his reflexes; he appeared to be deeply hypnotized. When he spoke, his words were slow and very low, but I could make out his answers. He began describing the day of his death.

"I am in a large hall. The men are around me. I feel very hot. I feel so hot, I feel quite weak."

"Were you wounded in battle?" I asked.

"No. I am ill. There is someone right next to me. He's talking to me. It's a monk."

"What are you talking about?"

"I'm frightened. I'm frightened to die. I want his blessing." Mark's voice had become nearly inaudible. Though he did not move in the chair, various expressions crossed his face. He looked both anxious and sorrowful. I decided to move him ahead quickly through the death experience.

"Now you have died. You will be able to see what they do with your body. Tell me what you see."

His voice was stronger now as he responded to my question. "I'm looking down. There is a procession of many people." He then looked surprised and said, "Oh! they're putting me in a wall."

I asked him to tell me more. "It's as though they carved a place in the wall, sort of like a shelf, and they put my body in it. Then they covered it with a stone."

Here was my chance to find out if there was a name connected with this experience. I reasoned that if he could see what was written on the stone, we would be able to get his name. "Can you see what is written on it?" I asked.

"Can't see very well, can't make it out. . . . Don't think I can read."

"Where is the wall?" I asked, wondering if it was in a church somewhere, or in a mausoleum.

"It's in the castle. That's all I can see." I realized that the death had been unpleasant for Mark but not because he had been slain in battle; apparently, he died of some disease. The problem appeared to be the Christian theology he had been taught and his fear of hell and devils. The monk beside him seemed to be the sole focus of his attention as he lay dying. Presumably he was confessing his sins to the monk. But was it only this fear of retribution that caused the feeling of sadness Mark had when he saw the castle in Italy? I decided to probe further.

"Now that you are dead, what do you feel about that life?" I asked him.

"It wasn't a very happy life. I was lonely. There was no one I was close to, and it seemed a hard life."

Because of the atmosphere of general sorrow and the fact that Mark's facial expression still showed unhappiness, I suggested to him that for a few moments he would have a pleasant and happy dream. I sent him far into his mind and told him that he would find deep peace and relaxation during this interlude of a happy dream. I was not yet ready to bring him out of the hypnosis, because I felt there was more to be discovered.

After a few moments I resumed my questioning. If he had died around 1460, and had lived in Paris in 1870, was there a lifetime in between? I decided to explore this. "Now you have come out of your pleasant dream. We are going back in time again. It is the year 1550. Do you see anything?"

"Just drifting," he responded.

"It is now the year 1650, do you see anything?"

Once again his answer was no.

"It is the year 1700, do you see anything?"

"I see grass."

By now I had hypnotized enough people to know that when they stop drifting and see something vividly, they are ready to report a past life to me. I asked Mark, "Look down at your feet. What are you wearing?"

"Nothing."

I probed further. "Are your feet bare?"

"Yes."

"Are you wearing any clothes?"

"Just pants. I'm near the sheep." Mark smiled vividly in his hypnotic trance, and added, "I like the sheep."

I knew he was barefooted, wearing pants, in a pasture with sheep, but I had no idea of his location. "Do you know where you are?" I asked.

There was a long pause, as Mark struggled to answer. Finally, he said, "No, don't know."

I tried again. If he didn't know where he was, maybe there were other people around who might give me a clue. "Are there any people around you?"

"No people. My sheep."

If I couldn't pinpoint any people or the name of a place, perhaps I could get a description of a landscape that might help. I was struck by the fact that when Mark was the French soldier, he seemed to know he was in Paris, but this shepherd in the 1700s didn't seem to have any knowledge of where he was. I asked, "Are there any trees or streams around?"

"The vines."

(After he came out of hypnosis he told me he had seen vines that looked like grapevines, but did not know how to describe them when he was under hypnosis.) I tried again. "Do you ever see any people?"

"Saw the master once." Ah, another person. Perhaps I could get some information now on where he was.

"What was the master's name?" I asked.

There was another long pause, as Mark seemed to struggle with the question. Finally he said, "Don't know . . . Master Jean, Jean, maybe." He pronounced the name in the French fashion, indicating that perhaps he was back in France now. His face brightened again and he volunteered, "The sheep feel nice."

When Mark was the French shepherd boy, his facial expression was quite different from that of the soldier in Paris and the knight in Italy. When I asked him questions as the shepherd boy, he frowned and struggled very hard for answers, but they were slow in coming. He showed animation only when discussing the sheep.

Because Mark had been under hypnosis for an hour, I decided to bring him out of the hypnotic state. He was given the usual suggestions that energy would return to his body and that he would feel relaxed and refreshed when he awoke. He woke up to the count of three, and carried out the posthypnotic suggestion I had given him as a test of the depth of hypnosis, which was to ask the time at the moment he awoke. I had not given him the suggestion that he would remember everything that occurred under the hypnosis, but he did remember some of it.

"You know," he said, "that business about the sheep. I had the feeling that I couldn't think very clearly. It was as though I was mentally retarded. I felt happy, but I didn't know the name of anything. I did have the feeling I had always lived there and that the sheep were my main friends. Strange . . ." Mark's voice trailed off and he smiled. "I would never have thought I had been mentally retarded in a previous lifetime. It felt so very different from the soldier; the shepherd seemed much happier, even though he didn't seem to know anything."

Mark was a college graduate who had traveled widely and had a knowledge of history superior to that of the average subject, which made it difficult to establish the validity of the hypnotic regression. Had he only imagined past lives under hypnosis? Was there any information in the past-life regressions that he could not have known about through his historical background?

There was very little to go on. I did check the Parisian life, and found that the uniforms worn by the French soldiers in that time period were blue and white. Mark had described the battle, and I discovered this corresponded with the time when the Paris Commune was established and there was street fighting in Paris. But could he have known about this through his own readings in history? There was nothing to check in the shepherd's life because he had no concrete information to offer. In itself, however, this was interesting. Mark knew about the 1700s, and he could have constructed a life with much more glamour as well as greater historical detail. Instead, all he talked about was sheep.

The life of the Italian knight offered me only a few bits of data to check. He had said that his title was that of "Graf" and I checked this. This was a title that meant "Lord," and is of Germanic origin; but "Graf" is too widely understood for Mark's usage to prove any recall experience. The place in Italy he described to me appeared to be on the borders of what is now Austria. In 1450 there was an entirely different map of Europe. What puzzled me most was the description of fighting for the "Holy Roman Emperor." On checking, there does seem to be some evidence that this was the term used at that time, as well as during that period of European history before the nation states were established. The evidence, far from conclusive, was merely suggestive that Mark might have actually lived these past lives. Mark himself was impressed, not with the historical knowledge he displayed, but with the emotions he experienced. For many hypnotic subjects, it is the emotional level of the experience that has meaning rather than its intellectual content. As I had not told Mark he would remember this regression, the incidents gradually faded from his conscious mind.

In looking back, I see now that these initial hypnosis sessions set me on the path that has brought me over two thousand cases of past-life regressions. Initially, I thought of these sessions as a mild secondary interest. At the time I was struggling not with the problem of whether past lives were real, but with the question of how to deal with the disturbed adolescents who were increasing in number as the drug culture proliferated. I had been working in therapy with adolescent girls at an institution and began to feel that the therapeutic modes I had learned and practiced for so many years were entirely inadequate for coping with the problem. Many of these young people needed a place where they could grow and develop, far more than they needed the "sit down and talk" type of therapy. I developed a plan for a group home that I felt would be more beneficial than the institutionalization that so many of the young people were forced into. Most of my energies were concentrated on establishing and funding such a home and working closely with the girls. I conducted occasional hypnosis sessions, but they were not my primary focus. I felt the real world deserved my attention.

I had continued to teach psychology over the years, one course a semester, and always enjoyed lecturing and the contact with students. I was teaching a course in Introductory Psychology at a nearby community college. When I came to the section on the psychology of perception, I lectured to my class on extrasensory perception, and I noticed that the students perked up and were full of questions. I thoroughly enjoyed this, because I had by now read the scientific literature on parapsychology very thoroughly and was excited at some of the new approaches that were developing in the field. My enthusiasm must have been catching, for the students participated eagerly.

Among them was a young housewife who was returning to college to complete her degree. She was taking two courses, my Introductory Psychology course and a course in journalism. When the class met after the Christmas holidays, this young woman had quite a story to tell. On the evening of my lecture on parapsychology, she had hurried home because she had a journalism assignment due the next day. The assignment was to write a news story about an imaginary news event. She had put it off until the last moment, so she sat down and dashed off a story about an imaginary airplane crash. She gave the flight number of the plane (401), the fact that one hostess survived while the other died, gave the date of the accident, and said that it took place in Florida. The next day she turned in her assignment and enjoyed her Christmas holidays.

When she came back after the holiday break, she went first to her journalism class. The teacher asked her to stay after class. She had been correcting my student's paper about the "imaginary" plane crash when the news came over the radio that an airplane crash had just occurred in Florida. The details of my student's journalistic assignment tallied very closely with the report on the radio. The date was one day off, but the three-digit flight number was correct. The fact that one hostess died and one survived was also in the news report. The teacher was shaken by this. She asked my student, "How did you know this was going to happen?"

My student was amazed and horrified. She had thought she was preparing an imaginary story, and it had come true. How had this happened? She looked at me anxiously as she asked this question.

I was as astounded as the journalism teacher. How indeed had my student known about it? I speculated that she had been in a hurry to complete the assignment, so that when she sat down and dashed it off, she was in a mildly altered state of consciousness. Her ego did not interfere, which was why she was able to write the story so quickly. Apparently, she had tapped in to a probable future reality because this was the easiest way to get her assignment done. I knew this was not really an explanation, but I could not think of a better one.

The students in the class were as impressed as I was at this evidence for precognition. It was an unusual case in that the material was written down and in the hands of someone else at the time the event actually took place. I felt that coincidence was ruled out because of the correctly reported three-digit flight number.

Unfortunately, the student who had made the precognitive "hit" became quite concerned. She had never had any experience of ESP before, but now felt that because she had correctly predicted one event, she must be able to predict others. She worried about her husband, and was afraid something might happen to him on the job. She begged him to stay home from work one day because she "had a feeling" that something would happen to him. He went to work anyway, and nothing unusual did occur. I felt some responsibility toward her because I had brought up the question of precognition in my class before her own startling example of it. Instead of feeling elated about her new-found ability, she was realizing that it made her life more difficult.

I have since discovered that this is often the case. Negative or frightening episodes seem to send out emotional wavelengths of greater intensity than pleasant events. For those who have opened themselves up to these energy waves, life can become difficult indeed. It's no fun to visualize murders, accidents, and catastrophes all around the world.

I talked with my student in a futile attempt to reassure her. Finally, I took an authoritarian approach, because I felt that as long as I evinced interest in her maintaining her ESP ability, she would be subject to these negative feelings.

"You're not really psychic," I told her. "You were just doing a double assignment in your college work. You were providing an example of ESP for my psychology class, and at the same time fulfilling your English requirement. I feel sure that this will not happen again, and that your life will return to normal."

This statement seemed to do the trick. She was much relieved at the idea that she had merely performed a school assignment, and was no longer "psychic." She stopped worrying that something would happen to her husband and relaxed. She brought a turkey to the girls at our group home to celebrate Thanksgiving. I think she found more satisfaction in helping me with the homeless teenagers than she had in being "psychic."

My student taught me two lessons. The first lesson was that ESP can indeed take place, especially if one is in a relaxed and receptive mood. The second was that being "psychic" is a two-edged sword. If there is nothing to be gained in the real world by being able to predict catastrophes, there is no point in tuning in to this particular wavelength. And it is very difficult to know whether an intimation of catastrophe is truly ESP or merely a form of worry. Because one can't make this distinction until the event happens, much anxiety is suffered for nothing. And even if one can correctly forecast a coming catastrophe, there is often nothing one can do about it. If the event is a personal matter, it may be possible to take steps to avoid the situation; but in many cases, the catastrophes that are seen through visions or in other forms of subconscious activity cannot be prevented. What if my student had called the airline and told them that a plane would crash in Florida on a given day? They would clearly have written her off as a "nut" and nothing would have been gained by it.

Although all of us occasionally have glimpses of the future, I feel very strongly that it is wiser to live in the here-and-now. If the future is preordained, what is the value of knowing it ahead of time? If the future can be changed by our own free will, there is no way to "foresee" it, because it is not yet set. In either case, we are alive to see what happens next. If all of us could know ahead of time all the experiences we are going to have, and the outcome of all of the problems we are undergoing now, we probably would not go through the experiences. Living our lives would be like watching a rerun of a Superbowl game, and hold about the same degree of interest. The element of suspense is a very important part of being alive. Just as we watch soap operas and competitive sports to "see how it comes out," so we live our lives from moment to moment with the continuing challenge of making our own future. The knotty question of what the future truly holds cannot really be established at this time with the knowledge we have. It is an integral part of our here-and-now, three-dimensional existence to wonder about the future but never to know for sure. The game goes on and the end is not foreordained.

Another result of my section on parapsychology in my Introductory Psychology course was a decision to teach parapsychology instead of my usual courses in Child Development and General Psychology. I was fascinated by it. My students were fascinated by it. I talked to the college, and they agreed to offer a course in parapsychology under the Adult Education Division of the college. For the first time, I acknowledged to myself that my interest in parapsychology, hypnosis, and ESP was more than a casual avocation. The time had come to bring it to the forefront of my attention and to devote my energies to it. My own future in parapsychology research was beginning to unfold.

3

THE SEARCH BEGINS

New adventures were beginning for me. I was not only to teach a course in parapsychology, but I was to go through a learning process in my own life as well.

I was surprised to find that my class was crowded with people from my area who apparently were more knowledgeable in parapsychology than I was. I had read the scientific literature, but many of my students were into aspects of the occult that were completely new to me. They soon discovered that I had very little knowledge of mediums, astrology, séances, and other aspects of occult exploration that had fascinated so many people for so long. I suppose this represented my prejudices. I believed that until so-called proper authorities investigated parapsychology, it didn't truly exist except as folklore. In this I may have been somewhat unusual; a great many people in our culture have had some contact with table tipping, ghost stories, or other aspects of the everyday occult. I've never cared much for movies or books on these subjects, and so found myself ignorant of the kinds of phenomena my students described to me.

One of my students brought a Ouija board to class, and had her daughter demonstrate the kinds of responses that can be obtained with it. I watched with interest as her daughter's hands flew rapidly across the board, spelling out messages from a purported entity from beyond. I was interested, but not unduly impressed. The little I had read about Ouija boards indicated to me that the subconscious mind of the performer was operative in producing the messages. The fact that so many of the messages came through jumbled when two people were at the board suggested to me that there was competition between the subconscious minds of the two operators, resulting in the confused messages. I was impressed with the speed of the Ouija board manipulation, but I didn't feel it was supernormal. I had seen typists using the touch system operate just as quickly. As to the messages that came through the purported entity from beyond, they seemed quite ordinary in content.

When I taught my class, I was introduced to the enthusiasm many people feel for the works of Edgar Cayce, which led me to explore the written material about this native American medium. I was immediately struck by the fact that Cayce's abilities were revealed when he was hypnotized to correct a persistent problem of laryngitis. This occurred in his first hypnotic session, and I was interested to note that the hypnotist told him he would be able to speak clearly and easily under hypnosis. Cayce did speak and, to the surprise of the hypnotist, described his own physical difficulties with the larynx and gave instructions for the correction of the condition. This was the first time that Edgar Cayce gave a "physical reading," and it was on himself. The phenomenon of diagnosing physical ailments by going into trance and describing the condition of the affected organs was to characterize Cayce's trance readings. I feel that the instructions given by his original hypnotist—that Cayce would be able to speak while in trance— are in part responsible for the Cayce phenomenon. Cayce was told that when he was hypnotized, he would speak easily and well; and he continued to do this several times a week for many years.

Cayce was able to enter the self-hypnotic state easily, and always spoke while he was under. Fortunately, he had a secretary who took down what he said under trance. I wondered whether, if all of us spoke easily while we were hypnotized, we would all eventually produce some of the same material that Edgar Cayce produced in his trance state. What I have read of the Silva Mind Control Program indicates that psychic diagnosis while in trance can be easily obtained from Silva Mind Control trainees; and in this respect their results do parallel Edgar Cayce's work.

Many of my students were interested in astrology. Like everyone else in the culture, I had read the daily horoscope in the newspapers, but, beyond that, had no awareness at all of astrological theory or practice. This ignorance has been gradually dispelled, though I still retain a certain skepticism about astrology as it is applied in the everyday horoscopes of people living in the here-and-now.

What began to interest me deeply was the *theory* of astrology. I knew just enough of the developing field of quantum physics to understand that force fields around objects tended to organize the atoms and molecules within the force field. It made sense to me that there were radiations, both in the solar system and in the universe, that probably did have magnetic field forces that could in turn organize and operate through the atoms and molecules of our bodies and brains. I still feel that developing evidence from many sciences awaits a unified theory explaining how matter is organized from quantum waves—and that when this theory does evolve, it will refer to cosmic forces from the bodies of planets as well as the gravitational field of earth. In this sense, I think there will be a meeting of astronomy and astrology through a deeper understanding of the organization of particles that make up the physical world. But such theory construction is far beyond my capabilities; I could just perceive it dimly enough to be aware that we should not close out the possibility that astrological forecasts are telling us something about the effect of cosmic radiation on the minds and bodies of human beings here on earth. My 1,088 data sheets include the sun signs of all my subjects, although I don't yet know how to analyze the sun sign in relationship to the past life reported.

My parapsychology class continued for eight weeks, and I learned along with my students. I shared with them the literature on many parapsychological experiments. They shared with me their own experiences in contacting their "higher selves," in exploring their own psychic powers, and in visiting psychic readers and mediums.

When the class ended, I felt as if we had just begun. I had continued to do a few regressions, but had not organized a careful research study into hypnotic past-life recall. I asked for volunteers to work with me privately outside of the college grounds in exploring past-life recall under hypnosis. Many volunteered, and I finally ended up with a group of eleven subjects who agreed to work with me each week in my private office. I looked forward to the experience of hypnotizing more subjects, because my research to date had opened up so many areas and I was so full of questions, to which I hoped now I would find some answers. I had selected my subjects on the basis of their emotional stability, maturity, and ability to respond to hypnosis, and I looked forward eagerly to the first meeting with one of my subjects.

My major question was: "Can I find any *evidence* to back up a past-life recall?" I had no idea at that time into what byways I was being led, nor what adventures lay ahead for the group.

The first of the eleven subjects whom I hypnotized went under easily. She reported a past life as a peasant in Russia in the 1700s, but I was unable to get any information from her that would make it possible to check whether or not she had actually lived in that time period. She was the first to give me a word in a foreign language. When I had initially regressed her to 1780, she described lying on top of a stove of some sort. I questioned this, because lying on a stove seemed a strange thing to do. Under hypnosis she grew impatient with me and said, "Stove . . . stove . . . yes, it's a—" and inserted a Russian-sounding word. On awakening the subject, I asked her if she remembered the word she had spoken in Russian. She thought for a minute, then said, "Yes. But I think I know that word. My grandmother was Russian, and I think I remember her telling me that word." Once again, my hopes of finding evidential material were dashed. I was struck, though, by the way in which her body had responded to the hypnotic suggestion. When she had been the old woman lying on top of the Russian stove (which turned out to be a long, low platform of stones, heated by a fire at one end), she described objects around her as being very blurred. Tears ran down her cheeks and she seemed to peer dimly around her. It turned out that I had chanced upon this past life when she was very old. Apparently, she had cataracts and could not see. Her other senses were active, and she described vividly tasting her food. The tears that came from her eyes during the initial part of the hypnosis appeared to be related to the cataract condition. When I regressed her to a younger age, the tears disappeared and she saw everything clearly.

Instead of providing an answer to a research question, this first regression in my new subject group brought up a new question. Why is it the body responds to the hypnotic suggestion as well as the mind? If hypnosis is suggestion, are many of our everyday body reactions the result of suggestions we give ourselves? This phenomenon, which I now call psychosomatic memory, was to recur in many hypnotic regressions, both group and individual.

The next subject I regressed was Anna. Anna had an interest in the occult, but had done very little reading in the field. I took Anna to the year 1770. Her eyelids moved rapidly, and I knew she was seeing some kind of picture in her mind.

She began talking and I realized that she was a hypnotic subject who was able to speak easily under hypnosis. This was important, because many of my subjects were too relaxed to be able to verbalize well when they were hypnotized, and it was like pulling teeth to get them to answer my questions. Occasionally I run across a subject who finds it easy to talk under hypnosis, and this means that I can get the kind of detail that is missing in the regressions of less verbal individuals.

"I see a spinning wheel. I'm in a room and I see the sunlight on the floor. I seem to be . . . I'm small. I'm a young child."

I moved her ahead in time. "It is 1780 now. What do you see now?"

"I see trees. I like the feel of the grass on my bare feet." Apparently, she was still a child, so I moved her ahead to 1785.

"What do you see now?"

"There are men walking by. I seem to have something in my lap; I think it's beans. I'm shelling beans. There's a lot of activity, people moving around. I think it's a picnic or something."

Anna was spontaneous in giving me her impressions, rather than requiring my questions in order to see things vividly. This was a promising sign. I decided to direct her attention to the people around her, hoping for more detail. "Do you see anyone there whom you know?" I asked her.

"I know that man. Oh, yes, that's my brother. He has on work clothes; he's talking to a man in a tall hat."

"Do you know where you are?" I asked her.

This question is very hard for subjects to answer. Although they are aware of sensory clues around them, they have difficulty when they are asked to come up with a judgment about what they are seeing, or to give names and dates. The subjects also report that my questions seem to be a bothersome interference with the experience they are having. I told Anna, "Listen and see if you can hear the name of this town."

She paused, then said that she heard the name. "It's Webster, Massachusetts. It's some kind of happy occasion. Like a celebration, or something like that."

I told Anna she would go back to her home and share the evening meal with her family. "Tell me what you see now."

"They're all sitting around the table. I'm bringing in a bowl of food. My father is reading some sort of . . . it's not a newspaper, it's too big for that. It seems like a roll of paper, with wood at each end. He is reading it, and I think it is—like, a proclamation."

I asked Anna, "Do you know what it says?"

"No. He isn't talking about it."

Anna seemed so perceptive at observing what was around her that I hoped I could get her name. I asked, but she resisted. I said, "Someone in your family calls to you. What name do they use?"

"Rachel. That's right, I'm Rachel." She was pleased to have

come up with her name. Hypnotized subjects do seem to have a need to please the hypnotist, and they often feel uncomfortable when their mind does not present them with the information being requested. But despite this eagerness to respond, they still tend not to summon up their names or the places where they live unless they are told to experience it through hearing it articulated by others in that lifetime.

I don't know any explanation for this recurrent phenomenon. When people are fantasizing consciously, names and places are usually the first things they describe. When they are hypnotized, this ability appears to leave them. They can report what they see, and what they hear, and what they touch and smell and taste. But when it comes to logical thinking, or thinking in words, they run into a block. This led me to the question of whether, when we are under hypnosis, we are dealing with areas of the mind that are not normally available to us in waking consciousness. The usual tools of consciousness, such as the use of words and recall for numbers, are difficult to come by under hypnosis, and other abilities come into play.

I continued with Anna, because she was a lively personality in this life recall, and she talked easily and freely of her experiences. I asked her to describe her home and its setting. She told me that they lived out from the town, in the woods. She described vividly the view from the window of the room where she slept. She then talked about going into town, and said she had heard others talking of a boy drowning at sea. The story of the boy drowning made her become aware that the town was near the seacoast and that she knew of ships and sailors.

I decided to see if she had any emotions about the boy drowning at sea. I asked her, "Were you going to marry him?"

"No. I marry John."

I wanted to see if Anna knew about the town where she lived after she was married to John. I told her that she was going to get supplies, and that she was on her way to get them. I asked how she was traveling, and she told me that they had a horse and a crude buckboard wagon. She and John were going into town. Then I took her back a little in time to find out what their house was like. I said, "Now it is the night before you come to town to get the supplies. Where are you now?"

Anna replied, "It's very pretty here. We're lying by the stream."

I thought that I had made a mistake. I wanted Anna to be in her house in that lifetime and she was describing an outdoor setting. I tried again. "Now you are waking up in the morning in the place where you slept last night. And you are going on now to get your supplies."

Anna stirred restlessly. "We're under the trees, by the stream. Sunlight is coming through the branches." It wasn't until Anna awakened from the hypnotic session that she explained the reason for her restlessness during this questioning period. "I knew that you didn't understand, but I didn't quite know how to tell you. The trip to town took a long time, and we had to sleep outdoors. It was a two-day journey from our land to the nearest town. I wanted to do what you said, and describe the house. But I couldn't. You told me that it was the night before we got to town. It was a strange feeling—I felt I couldn't get through to you, but it was very important to me to tell you the truth, and not just give you what you wanted to hear."

I have found this phenomenon again and again in hypnotizing subjects. Certainly, their responses are the result of the hypnotist's suggestions and they do respond immediately when you tell them to see something. But when I have misunderstood what my subjects have said, or my questioning is not clear, they will not change the image to suit my interpretation of what it is they are doing. This is truly strange. If past-life recall is the result of suggestion and occurs only in response to the hypnotist's wishes, why this attitude? Subjects have a strong desire to tell the truth under hypnosis. They become very concerned about the truthfulness of their answers, and will cling stubbornly and literally to whatever it is they are experiencing.

I took Anna to the day of her death. I wanted to know what

had happened to Rachel, and to Rachel's rather pleasant and peace-ful life in the countryside in Massachusetts. I told her, "Now you will move ahead in time to the day that you die in that life. Without experiencing any pain or fear, you will be able to describe what happens to you."

"I'm in the bed. The cover is a quilt." Anna's hands began moving restlessly, as though she were fingering the quilt. I've found that occasionally the body tends to act out what is being experienced, even though the hypnotic trance is deep and the muscles are very relaxed.

Anna went on, "I feel very weak. I'm so worried about my little girl. I'm dying, I know I am dying. I'm scared about what will happen to my girl and to John."

"Where is John?"

"He is here. There is a lady downstairs, came to help with the . . . help me have the baby. The baby's dead, I think. Oh! I don't want to die. I have too much I have to do here."

Anna's face was agitated during this description, and the sugges-tion was repeated that she would feel no pain or sorrow. She was then told to move ahead to watch the burial of her body, and told she would be able to describe what happened.

"Just John and my little girl and a few other people. They've dug a grave down by the barn on the side away from the house. It seems as though I am above the scene, watching from above. John is very sad. I still worry about my little girl . . . she's so small and I'm not there anymore to mother her."

This experience of sorrow at death because of duties unfulfilled also occurred in other regressions. The grief seems to be related to other people, rather than felt for the self.

As Anna seemed to like Rachel's life, I asked her, "What was good about that life?"

"I liked it. We had no possessions—just simple, crude things. But I was happy. There was a good feeling. I felt close to John. It was a happy life."

I brought Anna slowly out of the hypnosis, and told her she

would feel pleasant and relaxed when she woke up and that she would remember everything she experienced. When she awoke, she seemed surprised at what had happened.

"It seemed so very real. I was there and I could see and hear and even smell things. It was funny, because it was so hard to answer your questions. It was as though I had to stop the experience and come out of it a bit in order to answer you. It wasn't unpleasant at all, but I just don't know what to make of it."

Anna was the best subject I had had so far. She was able to speak clearly under the hypnosis, she reached a deep state quickly, and she was able to recall all her experiences vividly. Her life as Rachel was an interesting one, but there was very little we could do to check out the data. We did find there was a town named Webster, Massachusetts, in existence in 1800, but beyond that no evidential material emerged. I decided to try to move Anna ahead into a more recent lifetime, in which perhaps we could check the data. I asked Anna if she was willing to try, and she said she was indeed.

"I like being hypnotized. It's an interesting feeling, and I like what happens to me when I'm under." So we set an appointment for the next week to explore Anna's past lives in more detail.

Anna had been born in 1938, so in the next session I moved her back year by year through the twentieth century. She reported, "Just drifting," down through the years until I came to 1917. Then she described a living room. She was looking out the window of the house, but when I asked her to look around, she described the furnishings in detail. Her voice quality was different now from what it had been when she was Rachel, the early pioneer in 1800. She seemed intelligent, but had none of Rachel's liveliness. She appeared to be unhappy. As I probed further, she vividly detailed her feelings.

She was bored in the small town where she lived. She read from a newspaper masthead that the town's name was Westfield, New Jersey. She described her feelings of attachment to the house she lived in and told me how she herself had made the curtains that hung at the windows. I took her to encounters with neighbors and friends and into shops on the main street of town, and she was able to give me many details. She told me that she felt restless and dissatisfied in the life; wanting excitement, she found herself involved in a plot to sell World War I government supplies on the black market. She told me that her husband was in the army and overseas, but she expressed no strong attachment to him.

I explored her involvement with the black market. Her voice shook with emotion as she described her fear of being exposed and her shame at the thought that she would be accused of profiteering while her husband fought overseas. As I listened to her, I could empathize with her feelings. She talked about the hatred of Germans and the total involvement of her community in grandiose ideas of the glory of warfare. It seemed as though the moods, feelings, and attitudes of small-town America in 1917 came alive in my office. When I brought her to the death experience, I was shocked to find that she had killed herself.

"I put the gun to my head and then all I see are magnificent colors. I don't hear any explosion. Oh! I haven't escaped—I'm still aware of everything."

This was my first experience of suicide in a past life. As Anna described it to me, it was as though when she shot herself, she experienced no pain, but stayed conscious. She was outside of her body. She had the feeling she had not escaped anything at all: She was still aware and still filled with the emotions of shame and confusion that had led to the moment of suicide.

I was concerned about the effect this experience would have on the Anna of the here-and-now. Out of hypnosis, she said she was shocked at suicide, and hadn't thought of it in her current lifetime. "I've been unhappy at times, but suicide has never seemed to me to be a way out. Maybe it's because I know from this past life that it solves nothing."

Because she was able to give me so many details, and because Westfield, New Jersey, in 1917 was a place whose records could be checked, this regression excited me. For the first time I had an opportunity to get evidential data that might check out. I wanted to know if there was any way I could distinguish "real" past-life experiences under hypnosis from fantasy. Does our subconscious produce past-life impressions from scraps of our current life, in the way it creates our dreams? Or do these reincarnation memories under hypnosis reflect the real past?

I regressed Anna to that same lifetime on three other occasions. I pressed for the kind of evidence and data I could check, and I was rewarded by an outpouring of details of life in the small town. The name of the druggist on the corner, the description and name of the police chief, and the name of the town constable who had discovered the black-market plot were all reported explicitly. Anna talked about her home, which she said was on Mud Lane, and gave other street names and places. She described the great fire of 1896, and told how the fire bell rang in her schoolroom though the fire was blocks away.

I hurried to the small town of Westfield, fifty miles from where I then lived. The other members of our research group were as interested as I in seeing if the details checked. On my first trip to Westfield, I was happy to find that the local newspaper had been microfilmed to as far back as 1885. The newspaper solved the "fire bell in the schoolroom" puzzle. It reported that the fire bell rang in the school because that is where the only bell in town was. An old newspaper report was accompanied by a photograph of Captain O'Neil of the Westfield Police Department in all his mustachioed glory. He was indeed handsome, as Anna had told me under hypnosis. All the other details she gave me, such as the name of the druggist in 1916, also checked out. The only problem was Mud Lane, where the house was; the street directory did not list it. But then I found a newspaper report in 1924 that said that Mud Lane had been changed to Crestwood Drive when it was paved.

A problem arose when I tried to check Anna's burial in the local cemetery. I found the family plot and the headstones of named family members as she had described them, but there was no headstone for her. I checked with the cemetery records and discovered that there were two unmarked graves in that family plot, including one from 1917 that could have been Anna's. As she had been a suicide, perhaps the family had buried her very quietly. The details regarding her husband's service in World War I were verified, but I could find no record of her existence in the town directory or at the cemetery. Her husband's name was there, but not hers. Was she a figment of my subject's imagination?

When I reported my findings back in our small research group, everyone looked at Anna with new eyes. We all thought that she must have actually experienced this past life, because she expressed the emotions so strongly and because so many of the details checked out. Without realizing it, I found myself caught up in the group enthusiasm. Anna was pleased at all the attention she was receiving, and responded eagerly when the others suggested we stay together as a group to explore Anna's hypnotic powers in more detail.

In hindsight, I realize that I should have expected what happened next, but of course, if we knew the future ahead of time we would not live through it. I'm glad I lived through the experience that followed, even though the end result was less than happy. I learned to move with caution with hypnotic subjects, because consequences flow from every action. I had been taught to believe that I must beware of psychotic tendencies developing in hypnotized subjects, so I was alert to this possibility. I knew that many people active in the occult field felt that demonic possession was a danger when people were hypnotized.

In the past, people had often thought that psychotics were possessed by the devil, and I knew that this was not the case. I believed that all the "crazy" people I had worked with as a therapist had essentially made a choice to become crazy; so I therefore felt that mediums who were "possessed" by their spirits, believing this to be a possibility, joined in the game for reasons of their own and became "possessed."

What I did not realize was that ordinary human egos and the social needs of group members strongly affect the outcome of any research study. We are all too human, and whether we are members of a PTA bake-sale committee or in a group for psychic development, our human needs and feelings shape the outcome. It was not ghosts or devils, insanity or weird happenings that were to be feared. What was to be feared was the effect of social pressures on the ego of someone who was chosen by a group to be its medium or its leader, and the strange ways in which we human beings tend to produce, when we work together in groups, the phenomenon that we think comes from outside ourselves.

And so it was that when I thought I had my first case in which objective evidence checked out, I found instead that I was only beginning my search. I was now to enter a bypass. As ghosts and spirits, séances, charges of fraud, strange messages, and automatic writing began to appear, I learned far more than I ever anticipated.

4

SEANCES, MEDIUMSHIP, AND DREAMS

Our research group was excited by the results of the research on Anna's regression. I regressed others in the group, and all of them reported past lives, but none of these could be researched, except for Mike's. Mike reported a life lived in the late 1800s and early 1900s near Baton Rouge, Louisiana. I was finally able to get his name, which he gave as Lawrence Johnstone. Under hypnosis, he said he had enlisted in the army and been killed in France in 1917.

In researching the World War I dead from Louisiana, we did find an L. Johnston who might have been Mike in his past life. Suggestive—but not proof.

Anna, the star of our research group, suggested one night that we try table tipping, something she had done in her earlier years. The rest of the group agreed eagerly, and we began our experiment. There were nine in the group as we sat around my large dining table. I felt self-conscious, for table tipping wasn't my idea of para-psychological research; but I thought it might be intriguing.

The maple dining table rested on a vinyl tile floor, so it wasn't difficult for the table to move back and forth. We sat with our hands spread out on the top of the table, and Anna offered the "invocation."

"If there is anyone from the spirit world here, let them respond to us. Tip the table to the right for yes, and to the left for no."

We sat for several moments, tense yet interested in what might occur. Slowly, the table began to tip toward the right, slipping easily over the tile floor. Then it righted itself. We had had a response! We asked questions of the table, and for the first fifteen minutes the answers came very slowly indeed. Then I noted a phenomenon that was to occur throughout the rest of our table-tipping sessions. The table quivered beneath our fingers, jiggling up and down. I had a subjective impression that the table was growing lighter and highly responsive to us. I glanced under the table to see if anyone's knees might be operative in moving the table. We were crowded closely together, and I could not rule out knees as the cause of the phenomenon. The table moved rapidly up and down in a fluttering motion. Then we heard a cracking sound that seemed to come from inside the table. At first it was a small popping sound that would come and go intermittently as we asked the questions, but it then seemed to increase in loudness as the group's attention was focused more and more on the experience we were having. As we grew more involved in the procedure, the table seemed to become more responsive to us.

It is clear to me that the physical contact of our hands on the table was the cause of the table moving. It was not moving "on its own"—and yet . . . and yet . . . There are aspects to this phenomenon that could not be conveniently fitted into the physical explanation that came so easily to my mind.

The popping noise grew louder, until finally a loud crack was heard. Neither our hands on top of the table nor our knees under it could have caused this. I wondered about the heat generated by our hands. Was this heat being transferred to the wood of the table and having a physical effect within the wood?

The table gradually tipped out answers to our questions through a laborious process of spelling out the letters of the alphabet. The table would tip at the correct letter. As the group slipped into the spirit of the experience, the table moved faster and faster. We began guessing at the outcome of the laboriously spelled-out words, and the table indicated yes or no by tilting up or down. The group asked the name of the entity communicating with us, and the answer came through: "Ethan." Anna was pleased at this because she had told us she was pregnant and if she had a boy she wanted to name him Ethan. I paid close attention to Anna's hands on the table, but could find no special evidence to indicate that she was governing the movement at the table. There were eight of us, and it seemed that somehow we were responding as a group, rather than one individual's controlling the table phenomenon. I speculated that perhaps we were communicating telepathically, and using the table as a means of turning our group consensus into the "message" we wanted to receive.

The table game continued once a week for a month. The table became so responsive that one night one of its legs fell off and the table crashed to the floor. Like the rest of the group, I jumped up, startled. But then I reasoned that the table leg had been weakened by all of the tipping we had done, and that the table leg falling off was a natural phenomenon and not evidence of poltergeist activity.

Perhaps as much in the interest of saving my furniture as of developing insight into "communication with spirits," I suggested we try automatic writing instead of table tipping. Anna volunteered to be the automatic writer, and we began the experiment. We sat around my dancing dining table, mercifully quiet now, and I took Anna into a deeply relaxed state. I put paper and pen beside her and told her she would be able to receive messages and express them by writing. Anna picked up the pen and, very slowly, began to write. As her eyes were closed, one of us had constantly to turn the pages of the notebook, and it was difficult to understand the writing. I deepened Anna's trance, and told her that she would be able to write with her eyes open without coming out of the trance.

The words began to flow. The purported entity said that he was "Ethan," the entity who had answered our questions by table tipping. We asked Ethan a number of questions, some of which were answered and some not. One of the group asked: "Can you tell us who you were in a previous life?"

There was a long pause, then Anna began to write: "No." The questioner continued, "Did you know us?"

Anna's hand wrote faster. "In one way or another I knew all of you. You cannot yet, if ever, comprehend the dimensions in which you are trying to converse. Wait until you can understand. The cosmic psychic skills are beyond most mortal minds—the mind must be trained to go beyond now. Mike is learning and Anna is on the verge. Fear stops most."

The questioner continued, "Can you tell us more about you?" The answer came quickly this time. "I cannot tell you any more than you can tell me about your past. Someday you will comprehend." I was concerned that Anna's nervousness over her psychic ability might mean that she should not continue this automatic writing process. I asked the hypnotized Anna: "Should Anna continue to write in the presence of others?"

The pen hesitated, then scribbled rapidly: "She is afraid and, while fascinated, she is also somewhat afraid of others' opinion. I can keep going as long as she wills me. She does want to work with the group because people bring security and source of strength. Security is necessary to her now, especially as she is alone."

This initial exchange with "Ethan" set the tone for the four months of experiments to follow. The group would gather around each Thursday evening to ask Ethan questions and to watch Anna write the answers. It was good to have my dining table resting quietly on the floor again. I had had my doubts about whether any paranormal phenomenon was actually associated with the table, but, in truth, I did believe that some form of psychokinesis had been going on. Certainly, the knocks and raps on the table could not be explained by the action of any human agency, other than some sort of human radiation. The table movements also were difficult to describe in terms of ordinary physical movement. What did seem obvious was that, as a means of communicating with the unseen world, the table was a very laborious and unnecessary means.

As our group meetings continued, "Ethan" was asked questions about our practical, everyday lives. The temptation to find out what is going to happen in the next few weeks or months lies within all of us, and I suspect that whenever any "ghost" appears and seems willing to communicate with us, we are anxious to get some kind of fix on the future. Although the entity who claimed the name Ethan would occasionally answer our questions, more often he would describe philosophical ideas.

The group grew impatient with some of Ethan's evasions. Group members wanted some real answers, answers that could be checked out in the real world. Anna's pen, supposedly guided by Ethan, began to cooperate. The automatic writing indicated that Anna was pregnant, but that she would have an abortion or have a miscarriage, and he, Ethan, would not be born to her because of this. It was for that reason, claimed the automatic writing, that Anna was open to this spirit and could communicate through the automatic writing.

Ethan made several predictions other than those about Anna. Of his four predictions, one proved partially true, one completely true, and two never occurred. This seemed a poor batting average. Ethan often commented on how we were wasting time with questions about what would happen to each one of us in the short term future. Once he scribbled impatiently on the pad, "Enough of these parlor tricks! Let's get down to our real business."

In the course of the automatic writing sessions with Anna, the group began sorting itself out into true believers, moderate skeptics, and a small group that believed that what was happening might be the spirit possession described in books on the occult. Soon we were spending more time arguing over the phenomenon than exploring it. In an attempt to deflect the growing dissension in our research group, I hypnotized Mike again. I myself felt more comfortable working with Mike, because he had a scientific background and the material that came through him was from himself and not from a purported entity. However, after Mike had taken center stage for several group sessions, Ethan returned through automatic writing by Anna and said, "Anna feels left out unless she is participating through the writing. Soon I will be able to speak through Anna."

I pondered over this message. If Anna's subconscious was operative in the phenomenon (and I was sure that it was at least in part), it was apparently important to Anna that the focus again shift to her in our research group. At our next meeting, Anna began the automatic writing. Then she laid down the pen and, with her eyes closed, began to make strange sounds in her throat. After a few minutes of struggle, a voice finally emerged. It sounded much like Anna's voice, but was slower and deeper. Ethan had arrived and was speaking through Anna!

Later, Anna said she had no recollection of what she had been saying when she spoke as Ethan. Certainly, the communication was much faster than it had been by automatic writing. The content of the material also changed. Ethan was even less willing to answer our everyday questions when he was speaking through Anna than before. Instead, he would tell us about dimensions beyond the physical plane.

I listened with much interest and observed Anna closely when she went into the trance state. Her breathing was slowed, as it had been when she was under hypnosis. I could detect no essential difference between the mediumistic trance and the hypnotic trance. I noticed that there were no gestures or physical movements other than in the larynx, the lips, and throat. This again is typical of hypnotized subjects.

What did Ethan teach? In essence, the material that came through Anna was very similar to that coming through mediums all over the world. The difference in this case was that Anna did not communicate with other dead spirits or use Ethan as a spirit guide. Instead, when she went into the trance and began speaking as Ethan, we were all treated to a sermon.

I am aware that throughout the world there are mediums who are bringing forth material; and each assembled group is likely to believe that the ideas coming through in its hearing should be brought to the attention of the rest of the world. Often the "entities" say that a book must be written encompassing the material that has been revealed through automatic writing or mediumship. I believe that each of these groups brings forth the kinds of understanding and insights that its members are themselves reaching in the mundane world, and that these are expressed through one member of the group, who becomes the medium. In this sense, while I cannot disprove the presence of otherworldly entities, I think that what is emerging is a new form of understanding of our place in the universe. Each group learns in its own way; each leader teaches what can be understood in that group.

We all found the material interesting, but the group dissension continued to grow. There was much suspicion regarding Anna and the material that came from her, because some of it contradicted the beliefs of two members of the group. At one session, the most suspicious member demanded that Ethan tell us who he had been in his last lifetime, so that we could evaluate the material he was giving us. Mike and I felt that checking the credentials of a supposedly dead entity was a useless proceeding. If the ideas were interesting and useful to us, we could adapt them; if not, we could discard them. But because Mike and I were in a minority, the grilling of Ethan continued. At the next group meeting, Anna immediately went into trance and, as Ethan, reported her name and occupation in her most immediate last life. Ethan told us he had been a teacher of art in New York and had died in the early 1900s. He told us where we could look up his biography.

Oddly enough, this information seemed to satisfy some members of the group. I thought it was totally irrelevant. After Ethan had given his name, rank, and serial number to the skeptical group members, I learned that the group had been meeting several times a week without me for consultations with Ethan. By this time Anna no longer required any hypnotic induction to go into trance, and was clearly becoming a medium on her own. I continued to go to the meetings, but saw that the schisms within the group were changing its entire focus. A religious fervor appeared to take hold of the group when Anna went into trance and we listened to the "sermon." I was increasingly uneasy. This was certainly not my idea of parapsychology.

As the group was shifting and changing, and while Anna was coming into her own as a medium, things were happening to me— things I had never expected to have happen, and which I treated with great caution. I see now that I had decided to explore myself as a research subject because Anna was being preempted by other group members.

It had been easy for Anna to take up automatic writing. I reasoned that anyone who is hypnotized can be told to write automatically under hypnosis, and the subconscious will oblige. I decided to experiment with myself. By this time I had learned to use self-hypnosis. One night I sat down with pen in hand, put myself in a light trance state, and told myself that the pen would write without my control.

My arm picked up the pen and began to write. At first the writing was disjointed, but soon it began to flow easily. It took me several sessions before I was aware that the material was not coming from outside of me. While I was apparently blocking some sensory cues from my hand to convince myself my hand was moving through some outside volition, as I continued my experiments I realized that the ideas my hand were expressing were ones coming into, and being expressed through, my mind. This material was originating in my brain, and the *method*—the automatic writing—was simply a dramatic way of expressing it.

In this slight trance state, I seemed better able to express concepts than in my normal waking consciousness. I wondered how many books had been written by writers in a slightly altered state of consciousness.

I will quote a small portion of the automatic writing to illustrate the ideas that did seem to come through. They are not unique ideas, and I have heard them expressed much better by other authors, but this is what my automatic writing was like:

Tonight we must discuss the nature of reality in the plane after this, where you go when you "die." It is a homecoming, a celebration. You create much of it with your mind, but the important difference is that other minds are in harmony with yours. You only associate with similar minds, so you find obviously more harmony than in the fourth plane. [Apparently, this means three-dimensional reality.] In a manner of speaking, there is more segregation in the next plane, because like goes to like. You can create any semblance of earthly bliss or paradise you wish, but this often becomes boring and loses interest after a while. The major activity in the next plane is intellectual understanding. Many lessons are given to those interested, and preparations are made for many more creative acts. There are experiences above this plane that some get involved in. And this sixth plane is beyond the next planning stage. It is a preparation in what you would call world formation. In the most basic sense the universe is constantly being created—new galaxies, etc.

This process of creation is ever-expanding. Entities shape and form it, then split into smaller divisions of consciousness, act out scenarios, merge, separate, and recreate into infinity. The supernova that your astronomers see is a pale reflection of the creative unfolding that goes on at these other levels, because only light energy is perceived in the fourth plane. This creation is indeed the glory of God. The God concept is on its way out in the hierarchical sense. This is where the new religion will differ most from the old. Your concept of God was of a hierarchical "mover and shaker" who was also a caretaker. Jesus tried to alter this concept and tried to emphasize brotherhood. By this he meant that we were all cocreators of the universe, but the fourth plane was not ready yet for the concept, so you turned brotherhood into "Son of God." This was understood better in Atlantis, and before that in some primitive cults in some of the islands in the Pacific. Later it decayed, even in Atlantis, and was one of the reasons for attempting a new synthesis through the destruction of Atlantis.

Atlantean pioneers in Egypt tried to express this through numbers, but the concept became entangled in Egyptian tribal ideas of animal totems. Numbers are important beyond your understanding now. Mathematics is a form of music. In the plane beyond this, it is heard as harmonics.

You can get the flavor of the harmonies of the universe from certain music.

This, however, must be grasped intellectually and multidimensionally. Mathematics in your culture is very decadent, and hardly reflects at all the original multidimensional harmonies existing in many spheres and dimensions at once, plying them together without the need for space and time concepts.

In addition to giving voice to essays like the above, the automatic writing would come up with numbers and mathematics. Although I have some interest in this field, and have studied advanced statistics in order to do psychological research, I am primarily at home with people, not with mathematical concepts, so I surprised myself by producing algebraic formulas. I did have enough background in mathematics to formulate the appropriate letter and number values, so the phenomenon cannot be said to be supernatural. But I certainly didn't understand what it was I was writing down.

One night I produced a formula that related to vectors in space. The automatic writing indicated that if this formula were understood, it would be possible to find places in the "matrix of harmonics" that would enable us to trap power sources beyond those normally available in our particular space-time continuum. I took the formula, which contained about eight letter-number values, to a physicist friend and asked him to evaluate it. It certainly made no sense to me. I was afraid to tell him where I had found it, so I simply said that "someone" had come up with this and I wondered if it had any meaning. He said he could find no particular meaning in it. While it was not entirely illogical, he didn't think it made much real sense.

I have a hunch that a good deal of material like this is floating around the United States at this time. Parapsychological researchers are asked to evaluate automatic writing that comes in the form of strange-looking symbols, mathematical formulations, and purported languages that the automatic writer has no conscious awareness of. My own experience with automatic writing didn't indicate to me that anything was coming through that I myself didn't have the background to express in the form in which it emerged. The difference seemed to be that when I was writing in my ordinary consciousness, I was much more modest in my claims. It would certainly not occur to me to tell people what life after death was like, or to believe I had any true knowledge of it. Yet this is what came through automatic writing. You certainly can't prove through me that there is no point at which vectors collide and we can escape into the harmonics of a universe beyond space and time. I suppose it is at least intellectually possible to do this; but it would also never occur to me to come up with a formula for it, especially one that seems to have no practical application.

My experiment with automatic writing lasted about four weeks. I felt that although the phenomenon was interesting, there was danger that one could become absorbed in the activity to the detriment of whatever else one was supposed to or needed to be doing. Real life, I felt, should be the focus of my attention.

Interestingly, as soon as I stopped the automatic writing, my dreams suddenly changed. I had been keeping track of my dreams off and on for many years because this was one of the tools I used in therapy. I analyzed my own dreams when I was in training as a therapist, and I often analyzed my patients' dreams. The first dream I had that was at all out of the ordinary appeared shortly after I had first regressed Anna. I woke up around two in the morning and sat bolt upright in bed. The scene in front of my eyes was as vivid as though I were still sound asleep, though I was aware that it was a dream image, and not a "vision," that I was seeing. But it had an immediacy and reality that few dreams had shown me before. It was as though I had come awake or become conscious in the dream state, and this is why I was able to recall the dream so vividly.

I saw myself wrapped in a rough brown robe with a hood. The lower part of the hood was pulled across my nose and mouth because I was in an area of blowing sand. I was supervising the loading of strange-shaped boxes onto the flat surface of a cart with heavy wooden wheels. The boxes were oblong, with rounded tops. The cart was pulled by two small oxen with large horns. As I stood there checking off the boxes as they were loaded, I became aware that it was very important that we remove them from their normal location and store them, because some danger threatened the place where I normally dealt with their contents. I was aware that this was a library, though the materials were not in the form of books. I knew that I must get them to a safe place and see that they were preserved for posterity. In my dream, I knew that they related to my parapsychological investigations. The thought that flashed through my mind as I sat up in bed, the dream images still vivid before me, was, "Of course! I've always known about reincarnation! I have dealt with it often in past lives."

It took me about an hour to drift back to sleep. I was very impressed with the vividness of this experience, as I had seldom awakened in the middle of a dream before. I certainly had never had such a sense of conviction, the clear awareness, that the dream was sending me a message; most of my dreams are cluttered and disorganized and deal with everyday activities. But in the cold light of morning, when I awoke again, I put aside the thought of the dream. I reasoned that it could be explained by my current interest in reincarnation, and that therefore this dream, like the others, dealt with my everyday life. But that powerful feeling of conviction! I'd never experienced that before.

The next unusual dream came around a month later. This time, too, I awoke at the end of the dream and stayed wide awake for several hours. The feelings in the dream were so intense that I still had physical reactions to them an hour later. I could feel my pulse accelerating, and my body felt highly energized. Once again I finally dropped back to sleep, and awoke the next morning, again with a clear recognition of having had the dream. But in the morning the physical reactions were gone.

In the dream itself I found myself standing on what seemed to be some sort of ledge, but, oddly, I didn't seem to have a body— nor did the two other people who were with me, who seemed to be teachers of some sort. Our relationship was an easy and friendly one. I was telling them how much I enjoyed watching thunder-storms. They conveyed to me (I can't say they told me, because language didn't seem to be a part of the dream) that if I wished, I could feel what it was like to be the storm, rather than simply observe it. I agreed that this would be interesting, and instantly I found myself in what seemed to be the center of a raindrop. My consciousness was focused as part of a tremendous electrical surge of energy that was moving through the earth plane as a storm. I felt a rush of exhilaration as I moved with and participated in the energy of the storm. I left the raindrop and returned to the ledge with my teachers, and told them how delighted I was with the experience. How marvelous it is to be a part of these tremendous energy fields! This was the powerful sensation I awoke with. I sat up in bed and experienced again the tremendous surge of power in that rainstorm. There was more to the dreams than I can relate in words: It had to do with participating in many different forms of energy, not just the energy of having one's physical body in the here-and-now.

In the morning when I awoke, my everyday mind went to work on this interesting dream. First I thought in Freudian terms: Was the experience of being part of the rain an expression of sexual feeling? It seemed to involve my entire body, and to relate to being part of a larger energy form. It certainly wasn't sexual in Freud's terms. I wondered if Freud had ever dreamed he was a raindrop.

A third interesting dream came several weeks later. I had set an alarm to wake myself in the middle of the night, hoping to catch more of the delightful new dream series I was experiencing. When the alarm rang at 2:00 A.M., I awoke slowly and came gradu-ally up to consciousness from the deeper ranges of sleep. I was aware that I had been conferring with two other persons. I don't know where we were, and I didn't see the faces or bodies of the other two, but somehow I knew that we were very closely allied in some activity. In the midst of our discussion—or thought ex-change—the alarm had gone off. I was startled, and I looked at the other two and thought to myself, "Who am I supposed to be? Where do I go when I wake up? Oh yes—I'm pretending to be Helen Wambach." This dream amused more than startled me. Was I conferring with other portions of my larger entity? Or was I undergoing something like Eve's experience in the *Three Faces of Eve?* I had been disoriented only for a split second, and had felt irritation at being interrupted during an important planning session.

Several other dreams that followed seemed to move down the same pathways opened up by my automatic writing. In one dream, I was shown what nurturance is, and the images ranged from the microscopic to the way in which worlds are cradled. It seemed to be a lesson in microcosm-to-macrocosm, and I was able to see and understand both orders. This dream carried little emotional content with it, however.

The final dream in the series was the most remarkable. Reciting it now makes it sound very bland, and it is difficult to understand how such a dream could have had such a lasting effect. I had been thinking before I went to bed about the problems of one of the emotionally disturbed adolescents with whom I had been working. She had gotten into serious difficulties and I found myself sitting down and writing her a letter. It was different from the automatic writing: I said nothing very important in the letter—it was merely a personal wish for her happiness and a belief that she would succeed in overcoming her problems. No big deal. But I hadn't intended to write the letter and seemed in a slightly altered state as I wrote it. I went to bed immediately afterward, and woke up several hours later with a feeling of almost indescribable bliss. In the dream I was flying very high in the sky. I was moving rapidly upward through what seemed to be the atmosphere of earth into a region where the colors were of magnificent intensity. I had a feeling of absolute freedom and beauty. That's all the intellectual content I can remember, but the feeling—oh, that indescribably beautiful feeling!

Although I can still remember faintly my sensations of deep happiness and peace, they have faded almost entirely from my awareness. I do know that for several months afterward my state of mind was remarkably calm and I felt a kind of happiness I had not experienced before. No wonder the mystics call it "beyond words."

While I was continuing my explorations into the recesses of my own mind, each member of the group was playing his own game in his own way. We saw each other seldom now, except for Anna and several of the group members who had become rather dependent upon her mediumship.

Then one day I got an angry phone call. One of the members who had been highly suspicious at the beginning, and then been converted to belief, had found out that Anna had lied to her. She had not had a miscarriage nor had she been pregnant, though she had told the group that both these things had happened to her. The medium had lied! She was indeed, then, possessed of the devil! The entire group was shocked by this discovery. It dissolved, and Anna never got in touch with me again.

What had happened? Was Anna's entire regression through her life in Westfield also a lie? I knew she told me that she had an aunt who had lived in Westfield, so I thought it was within the realm of possibility that she had heard some of the details of small-town life there when she was much younger. Still, I continued to believe there was no evidence of fraud in the initial regressions.

When I looked back through the material to try and understand what had happened to Anna and what had happened to our research group, the answers leaped out at me. After our initial phase of hypnotic regression to past lives, when Anna had begun the automatic writing, Anna's subconscious had written through Ethan: "Anna is afraid. She wants to be a part of the group and needs to be part of the group, but she is afraid."

So Anna had predicted the outcome of her experience as a medium. Even her initial regression as the girl in Westfield indicated shame and fear of being "found out." The group member who so intensively quizzed Ethan because she feared possession by evil spirits had had her belief system strengthened. Anna had reinforced her belief that she was someone who could not be trusted. So in the end, the best predictor of our group's research results were the conscious feelings of all the parties concerned. We had set about initially to search for evidence of psychic phenomena. We then began to search for "ultimate truth" and accepted a teacher. Poor Anna was pressured by the group's need for her to be a perfect teacher, and when the group delved into Ethan's abilities, Anna predicted things that she could pretend came true. In that way, the group would accept her mediumship. The fault lay not in the medium, but in the way in which all members of the group began to take from the group that which they themselves wanted. We each made our own reality out of the psychic research group; and in the end, we were left not with absolute truth, but facing once again the reality of our own inner lives. The fault, dear Brutus, lies not in our stars but in ourselves.

5

MORE PAST LIVES AND MORE EVIDENCE

My experience with myself and Anna did not convince me that automatic writing represents thoughts from "spirits beyond our plane." The evidence of my dreams was somehow more intimately mine than the automatic writing had been. The emotional certainty, the feelings of bliss, and the vividness of the experiences made the dreams guideposts in my own emotional development. But that had nothing to do with their objective validity. I still wanted to get some kind of a handle on the question: "Are these experiences purely mental, or do they reflect the real past as we all know it?"

One case is not enough to prove that we have all lived before. I needed much more data in order to come to even a tentative conclusion on how to distinguish fantasy from reality in the past-life recalls. When I reviewed the thirty cases I had explored so far, I discovered that half of my subjects reported at least one brief lifetime in which they died before the age of five. Of all the information I had gotten from past-life recall under hypnosis, I felt this was the most important. It was hard for me to understand why people would fantasize being born and then dying within a few years. I did know that the infant death rate in the past centuries had been quite high; in primitive societies, nearly 50 percent of the infants died before reaching the age of five. I decided that the best way to establish past-life recall was not to put one especially psychic person in the role of "star" and try to prove one particular lifetime of theirs as conclusively as possible. Instead, I decided to gather a large group of subjects together and explore systematically certain phenomena about the past that I knew to exist, and to see whether my subjects would reproduce them.

Several events in my personal life brought me to the West Coast around this time, and a series of coincidences (Jung called this synchronicity) led me to the San Francisco Bay area, where I could most effectively pursue my researches. I began my new series by hypnotizing an additional twenty-five subjects, this time taking each of them from 1400 to the year 1945. My goal was to check out all available data from these subjects to determine whether they reported accurate historical data, and to see if any pattern emerged.

But the work was very, very slow. I tape-recorded each session; then each session had to be transcribed and the typed data given to a student researcher. It took many sessions to bring my subjects back through the average five lifetimes covering this span of 1400 to 1945. After a year of work, I realized that it would take me the rest of my life to collect the hundred cases I felt I needed to provide some sort of statistical certainty about the past-life phenomenon. Surely there must be an easier way.

I discovered that it was easier to get my subjects to describe their experiences while in a past life if I told them they didn't have to speak under hypnosis, but would remember vividly everything they had experienced when they awoke. I gave them the posthypnotic suggestion that they would want to discuss in detail what they had seen, felt, heard, and experienced in the past life. This procedure was an unqualified success; in fact, the problem often was to get the subject to stop talking after he had come out of hypnosis. I obtained a wealth of material as a result of my new method, but it was difficult to organize it reliably and in a way that lent itself to careful statistical analysis. I had hit upon the idea of going only to specified time periods, and that had worked; and I was gradually learning to limit the questions I asked subjects under hypnosis to the areas I wanted to explore. But even then my subjects gave me more than I cared to know. The transcripts of the sessions grew longer and longer, and it was more and more difficult to make sense of all the material I had on hand.

One of my very best subjects was Betty, a pleasant middle-aged woman with remarkable psychic abilities. I regressed Betty to a series of five lives lived between 1400 and 1900. All but one of these lives were humble, and there was no chance of finding recorded data to support her recall of them. However, she reported a life as a historical person in the mid-nineteenth century.

I said, "It is now 1840. Do you see anything?"

"I'm on a ship," she answered. "I see the ocean, the railing of the ship."

I carried Betty further into the shipboard experience and found that she was going to Russia. She described some of her experiences there. When I moved further into that lifetime and asked her to describe an exciting event, she said, "It's a message or something. Something from Queen Victoria. It's something very important." She was unable to give any more details. However, she was able to describe her childhood and law training in a small town in Pennsylvania. Although she puzzled over dates when I asked for them, her recall was excellent when I took her to specific time periods.

In attempting to find the date of her birth, I regressed her to 1798. She reported that she was about four years old, and described the small log house she lived in and the view of the countryside. We later discovered that her actual date of birth did indeed correspond with her recall. She was also able to give the year of her death, which she said was 1868.

When I took her to her life when she was twenty years old, she described herself as being in a small town in Pennsylvania and studying law. I asked whom she was working with in the study of law and she uttered the name "Mr. Wentworth."

My subject went on to give vivid descriptions of Washington, D.C. When I asked her to go to a pleasant event in Washington, she described a social occasion in 1841, and reported that she was at a musicale where a new tune, "Jingle Bells," was being played. Although books differ on the date of the original publication of "Jingle Bells," records do indicate that it was being played in 1840.

It was difficult for me to get the name of my subject. I finally took her to a time when she was looking at her name written on an envelope. She "read" her name as James Buchanan, Esq.

As Buchanan, she seemed very articulate and informed, in contrast with the personality she exhibited in earlier lifetimes. Buchanan reported that the purpose of his life was to demonstrate that single-minded devotion to work and high ambition could result in high achievement. But he paid a price for his success. Betty said that as Buchanan she was lonely and had little affection in this life. She expressed deep emotion at the death experience, tears coming to her eyes as she was brought to the deathbed.

"Now I am ready to die, and I want to see Elizabeth again," Betty (Buchanan) said at this point. "I do hope I see her."

Elizabeth was Buchanan's fiancée, who had died after their engagement was broken off early in Buchanan's career. My subject correctly gave her last name as Coleman. Buchanan's biography gives her name as Ann E. Coleman rather than Elizabeth Coleman. Most of the other details checked out. As Buchanan, Betty was studying law in a small town in Pennsylvania, as she reported. However, the name of the man with whom Buchanan clerked differed from the one Betty gave under hypnosis. She did give the names of the candidates for President in 1824 and 1830, though she reported that one candidate was running for office in 1832 and the records show him running in 1836. Interestingly, she did not go to the period in Buchanan's life when he was president. At the time when I was regressing her I didn't realize that Buchanan had been president between 1857 and 1861, the period in which the nation moved close to the Civil War. My subject was more involved in Buchanan's emotional life and didn't demonstrate any direct interest in the current issues in the United States in the 1850s. In part, this is because I didn't question her on these topics. I find that my hypnotized subjects will go to precisely what I am questioning them about; they seldom volunteer material outside of the experience being queried.

Betty was surprised at her experiences as James Buchanan. She denied any interest in American history and said she had not read anything about Buchanan. It is, of course, possible that she might have been taught something about Buchanan and had this information in her subconscious. But it's quite a feat to be able to produce this kind of information, acquired many years ago, and weave it into a past-life recall with very few errors in dates, names, and places.

At last I had a subject reporting a life that could be checked. This was exciting, and the results of our attempts to verify details were also exciting. It was a temptation to continue regressing Betty and get more and more information about her life as Buchanan. But she was nervous about the regression experiment because she didn't want to be another Bridey Murphy, with all the attendant publicity. Remembering what had happened with Anna, I understood her feelings.

I was equally interested in how the life of Buchanan fitted into the pattern of Betty's other lives. Betty had reported a life as a poor Pakistani native in the 1400s. Out hunting one day, the native was attacked by a wild boar, which injured his leg and crippled him. Since his family was too poor to support a cripple, he became a beggar and died of starvation several years later. In this lifetime, Betty's responses to my questions were slow, but her facial expressions and bodily movements were quite striking. When she went to the time of the boar's attack she grimaced and pulled her leg up awkwardly. Throughout the rest of this regression, she held her leg in this painful, contorted position.

In the next life to which Betty regressed, she was a woman in England in the 1600s. I first tapped into that life when she was fifteen years old. She was despondent because she had just escaped from a fire that destroyed her home and that of many others. (Was this the great fire of London in 1666?) Because all other members of her family died in the fire, she was apprenticed to a tavern keeper, and thereafter led a very difficult life as a barmaid. Although her personality as a feisty wench who fought for herself came through, she was repeatedly abused and mistreated, and eventually died, very painfully, after being raped and beaten by several drunken men.

The interesting aspect of this life as a barmaid was that Betty experienced considerable emotion about it after she came out of the hypnotic session.

"You know, I smelled the alcohol on those men," she said. "And I felt the same feeling that I've had in this life. In this life I haven't really known anyone well who is an alcoholic, but I've always been unusually afraid of people who are drinking. Now I feel I understand why. It's because I died at the hands of drunken men in that lifetime."

Apparently, the life as a barmaid immediately preceded the life as James Buchanan, and there were no other lives in the interim. What a contrast in lives! And what a contrast in personalities. Betty, who in real life is quite soft-spoken, spoke in a loud voice and crisply described everything around her when she was a barmaid, but her vocabulary was limited. When she became Buchanan, her voice changed and she answered my questions very matter-of-factly. She seemed more intellectually able and emotionally distant as Buchanan.

Because I was most curious to know if there was a lifetime between the one as James Buchanan and her current life as the wife of a rancher in California, I moved her through the years from 1868 to 1900. In 1902 she reported, "I see trees." I explored what she was experiencing with her, and it turned out that she was a young infant strapped in a leather carrying basket, propped up next to a tree. However, when I progressed her to 1903, she was no longer alive. Realizing she had died, I took her to the death experience. I asked her to see a map that would pinpoint the place where she had lived that life.

It was Florida that she saw, and she became aware that she had been born into a Seminole Indian tribe. It is intriguing to think that a president of the United States during the time when we were conquering the West and destroying the Indian tribes would be reborn as an Indian. What kind of karmic connections did Betty's series of lives represent? Certainly there was no simple pattern visible. It was necessary to explore further.

Another very interesting series of lives was provided by Shirley Kleppe, one of the students at a university in northern California who were assisting in my research. Shirley went under hypnosis easily, and from her I was able to get a consecutive series of lives, together with some impressions of the between-life periods.

Initially, Shirley found herself in Central America in the 1400s. In this lifetime she was an athlete, and she described in much detail a ball game played in a stone court—how the hoop through which the ball must be thrown was set at right angles to the playing court. (I was able to verify this information later.) The man in this lifetime was a cruel person. Grown too old to be a professional athlete by the age of twenty-four, he then took on the job of recruiting young men from nearby villages to become ball players. He was a harsh taskmaster to these boys, and felt after death in that lifetime that he had refused to understand the emotional and physical needs of others around him. He died at age forty.

Shirley next found herself as a black native in New Guinea in the 1500s. This life was very distressing. She lived in a very small village, and all the other villagers were terrified of evil spirits that lurked around them. Even to go into the woods required ritual incantations at various stones and trees along the path. She said that she was a member of the "lizard totem," and explained, "We are lizards because the gods will not be so angry with us if we choose a humble animal to represent ourselves."

As the New Guinea native, she died an accidental death at an early age. It was difficult for her to go to the death experience, apparently because the fears of that life were so intense that she did not want to reexperience them under hypnosis. As soon as we took her to the experience after death in that life, her facial expression relaxed and she expressed much joy at being free of the lifetime:

"God! That was a terrible life. We seemed to have no freedom at all and we were always terrified. Now I understand why some people are so against witchcraft. You can psych yourself up and find living nearly impossible if you get too involved with the idea of spirits."

She said that the death experience as a native was especially satisfying because as soon as she left the body, she became aware that all the ideas she had had during that lifetime about the afterlife were wrong.

After the early 1500s, Shirley reported a series of European lives. She also switched sexes, being born a woman in 1540 after at least two lives as men. She found herself in Italy, where she had a pleasant life as a middle-class housewife in Venice. This life was long and happy, because of her friendly family and the many exciting things going on in Venice. She described in detail some of the art works around her—which she could see because her husband had something to do with a studio or workshop—and also her clothing. We were able to verify later that the outfit she wore was the typical clothing worn by a middle-class female in Venice in that time period. I asked for names, and she gave them to me, although she felt they might not be accurate. She called her husband Andrea, and thought her own name was Leah Massachia.

At her death in that life she described herself as quite old and very willing to go. Her family, gathered around her, was crying, and she wanted to reassure them. She described her death experience as follows: "As soon as I get out of the body, I want to tell them that I'm fine, but I can't reach them. Then it seems as though I am going somewhere. It's almost like being pulled somewhere. The feeling is like a subway, I'm going through a tunnel and there's a lot of white light, hazy white light at the end of the tunnel. Then when I get through the tunnel on the other side there are friends who meet me. It's really nice."

Shirley was next alive in 1728, when she was again a female, and she located the area where she lived on the coast of the lower part of Normandy. Her name was Marie, and, as a very young child, she was happy with her parents. However, later in her childhood something happened to her parents and she became a servant in a tavern or inn of some kind. She saw herself vividly at that time (1750), dressed in a "funny-looking hat," black shoes, and a skirt of coarse cotton cinched in with a wide belt. Looking out, she saw the house across the street, which had leaded glass windows and was off-white in color. The house was wooden and the streets were cobblestoned. She felt in some danger from her woman employer, but had friendly feelings toward the man. When I took her to the day that she died, she expressed great fear and agitation. She said she was walking down a path in a forest when suddenly a number of townspeople carrying torches broke out of the forest. She knew that they were very angry at her, and she ran desperately for her life, but they cornered her and she jumped off the cliff.

I took her quickly to the death experience, and after she died I asked her to think about why she was chased by the townspeople. She reported that in that life she was a "sensitive" who was very close to animals. After she tried to heal a boy in the town, but he died anyway, the townspeople felt that she had put the evil eye on him and were going to burn her for witchcraft.

The more Shirley talked about this experience under hypnosis, the more relaxed and accepting she became. After she awoke from the hypnotic session, she described a feeling she had frequently had before and which she recognized when I took her to her death.

"I've often had a kind of 'spell' that has been difficult for doctors to diagnose. Sometimes I get this dizzy sensation and the feeling that I have to run. I've always just called it a 'spell.' "

A year later Shirley told me that she had never had a recurrence of the spells after this hypnotic regression. It is quite common for my subjects to tell me that after they have experienced death in a past life, a phobia or symptom they have had has gone away. Not surprisingly, Shirley felt the experience of hypnotic regression was very useful to her. She wasn't sure whether her hypnotic recall was fantasy or not, but as long as it removed her symptoms, she really didn't care.

Nevertheless, the death as Marie upset her, and she had no "life experiences" from 1754 to 1808. She said that she again entered life in 1808, as "Josh," a young redheaded boy, but that she lived only until 1816, reporting this death as caused by smallpox. In this lifetime Josh was in the United States, "somewhere between the East coast and the Mississippi."

Shirley reported one more life—from 1888 to 1916—between her life as Josh and her life today as Shirley Kleppe. During childhood in that life she found herself in a Norwegian fishing village, and left the village at about age fifteen to sign on as a common seaman on a vessel that traveled between Scandinavia and the United States. Vividly she described scrubbing the deck and seeing her feet turn red in the cold as she stood in the puddles of water on the deck. Her life as Lars, the sailor, was very uneventful. She described several East Coast ports, including Providence, Rhode Island. Lars lived in a small rooming house in Providence, and died of an unspecified disease at the age of twenty-eight.

What kind of karmic pattern emerges from Shirley's lifetimes? Again, it is difficult to see any progression. If you include her current life as Shirley, she reported three female lives and three male lives. She experienced life as a Mayan Indian, a black Guinean native, a blond Scandinavian, and an Italian and a French woman. In none of these lifetimes was she wealthy or important, but in none of them did she suffer from malnutrition or live in deep poverty.

The only theme I could find running through some of Shirley's lives was the involvement with witchcraft. As the New Guinea native, she experienced many of the negative aspects of superstitious beliefs about the afterlife. As Marie, she was subject to persecution because of the townspeople's beliefs about possession. Could her interest in parapsychological phenomena in this lifetime be traced to those two experiences? The unpleasantness associated with both those lifetimes would suggest that she would want to avoid psychic explorations in her present lifetime. But as the Italian housewife, as the Mayan ballplayer, and as Lars, the Norwegian seaman, there appeared to be no involvement in anything other than everyday life. And what of the life as Josh, the boy who died at the age of eight? What purpose did this serve karmically? There were certainly more questions than answers to be derived from these series of regressions.

My best hypnotic subject was Robert Logg, a San Francisco businessman. He had learned self-hypnosis in his early twenties while in a Veteran's Administration hospital, where he was diagnosed as dying of tuberculosis. He had found that using self-hypnosis to relax himself began to reverse his lung condition, and he gradually improved, to the point where he was discharged from the hospital as cured. (This is a remarkable example of how self-hypnosis can be used to develop contact with the subconscious levels of personality. Bob had brought himself from the very edge of death back into this lifetime.) He continued to use self-hypnosis through his college career, and the skills he developed served him in good stead for many years. It is perhaps through his experience with self-hypnosis that he began to realize he was having "psychic" flashes, which led him to study parapsychology, although he shied away from the more dramatic, "show business" aspects of psychic explorations. He came to a lecture of mine and felt strongly that he was to work with me in exploring the hypothesis of reincarnation.

The first time I hypnotized Bob, I realized that I had a very unusual subject, one of the very small percentage who could speak easily and well while in the hypnotized state. He seemed able to hold his consciousness at two levels, getting impressions from the deeper layers of the personality but able to relate them easily through the conscious mind. In our many hypnotic sessions, Bob has shown the ability to write hieroglyphics while in the hypnotized state and to speak foreign languages. We are still evaluating this material.

With Bob, I explored fourteen past lives. The dates of these lives are somewhat confused, because Bob often found the numbering system in our human concept of time difficult to deal with when he was in an altered state. He occasionally gave overlapping dates, but in general the time period was precise enough to allow checking of some data.

His most impressive and powerful past life was in Egypt, around 2000 B.C. He said his position was that of a high priest, but he himself did not feel religious. His primary job was to expand trade routes, and to arrange terms with neighboring tribes and bring about a peaceful exchange of goods and services to replace the warfare that had gone on prior to his rise to power. I asked Bob to give details about the non-Egyptian peoples he dealt with around 1900 B.C.

One tribe, which he called the Kawakanish, he described as "a rather aggressive Semitic, light-skinned people living in the region to our northeast, who specialize in livestock raising and the production of rye and popa."

"What land lies to the east behind this tribe?" I asked him.

"The lands are controlled by the invaders from the far continent. They adorn themselves and are rather artistic in the use of winged bull-like creatures. I believe the name is Assyrian for this highly developed civilization. Our Phoenician allies are constantly in fear and confusion from these land-based aggressors."

"Are there any slant-eyed people in your country?"

"There are slaves who were brought to our kingdom in an earlier conflict. We have slant-eyed yellow-skinned individuals who are considered poor in their work attitude. We call them the Skitchnia."

I asked Bob if he knew of any different races in his area.

"The peoples who brought the knowledge are long-headed people. They have elongated ear lobes and rather strange noses. There are very few of them left, and they are mostly a matter of legend. But there are a few still in the population. They are the long-headed people of the olden times."

Bob gave many details about his life in that time period, and we are continuing to check whatever data can be checked from four thousand years ago. Thus far, Bob's information about clothing and artifacts have proved accurate.

The second of Bob's fifteen lives was lived around 1300 B.C. and was in startling contrast to his life as a high priest, for in this lifetime he was a driver of a cart that brought grain to some central storehouse in Egypt. He lived in a small adobe house with a young wife and seemed to have little interest in the world around him, though he was aware of a new group of slaves, who had just been brought to the central granary. His major emotional impression in this life was his terrible sorrow at the death of his young wife; he reported that she had been bringing meat back to their dwelling when she was set upon by a pack of dogs and killed. He lived out the rest of his life in loneliness.

In these two early lives Bob had been male. In his next life, around 400 B.C., he was again in Egypt, but this time he was a woman of a merchant or trading caste, and was involved in intrigue centering around the throne. As a woman, he married someone of higher station—though not the Pharaoh or one of his direct relatives—and schemed to siphon off wealth from the royal household to the family he had belonged to before he married. The woman he was in this lifetime was cold and materialistic, becoming enraged when her husband died without leaving her any power or influence at the court. But, she reported, "My family now has influence, because they now have money. I'm tired of this struggle, it was all for nothing. The battle has been lost—lost—lost; the struggle is lost."

When I asked her how her husband had died, she responded, "A very ignoble death, of a common malady, and I shall take the noblest means to follow."

I asked Bob to see this body after death, and he said, "My body is treated as it should, with due respect to my status, and it is properly processed and placed with my chosen one. We are in an antechamber to the east of the main chamber in the cave of Kurakama."

The fourth life that Bob reported—as a male again, but this time in western Lebanon—was a very happy one for him. He had a wife whom he felt warmly toward and five children (he was particularly attached to one son who had a physical disability). His job was making cheeses from goat's milk and distributing them on the trade routes that ran through his small village. He was also very interested in the Jewish religion and said that his village had no rabbi, but that his father, whom he deeply respected, served as a kind of common-law rabbi and counseled the others in the village. In this lifetime, Bob conducted himself with great dignity and spoke in a thoughtful and solemn manner. He apparently enjoyed the position of prosperous tradesman in the village, and he was very attached to the land, which he described as remarkably beautiful, with trees and rolling hills. In this lifetime he died when a very old man, surrounded by his family and full of feelings of satisfaction about a life well lived.

Although he was again a male in his fifth life, everything else was very different. The time was around A.D. 100, and Bob found himself in Greece, orphaned at an early age and the ward of a powerful Roman governor of Greece. His relationship to the older man was sexual in nature. Bob described this life as sensual and pleasurable, but he had no feelings of accomplishment. He died of a disease when fairly young.

There is a long stretch of time from around A.D. 100 to A.D. 1300 that Bob and I have not yet explored, since he has not gone spontaneously to lifetimes in this time period. The next life he reported was as a woman in A.D. 1300, living a very primitive life in a village in Central America. The family village was small, and apparently there was no one to marry because intermarriage among the villagers was forbidden. So it was with considerable pleasure that the woman of this lifetime reported a raid from a neighboring tribe when she was sixteen, in which she was captured and married to one of the invaders. There was much enjoyment reflected in this account; being a captive apparently was much better than staying in the isolated family village. By age twenty-five in that lifetime, this woman already had several children and was contentedly living in a village on a river. She described thatched huts that sat on stilts over the water, and said that her favorite occupation was weaving bamboolike shoots. But when she was twenty-eight, an epidemic broke out in the village, and she died of a fever. Everyone else was also ill, and apparently the entire village was wiped out in this epidemic.

In Bob's seventh life he was again a woman, this time in Portugal in 1450. The woman of this lifetime lived in modest circumstances and had a peaceful though rather short life. She described vividly the town square of the city she lived in. She too died of illness, but was unable to tell what the illness was. Apparently, she was in a coma when she died, because she found the time of departure from the physical body difficult to pinpoint.

After two lives as a female, Bob was a male in his eighth life, in the 1500s. This time he returned to a higher status, being an Italian nobleman in a village just south of Naples. But it was a cold and unsatisfying life. He seemed to have little with which to occupy himself, and he felt "turned off" by the other noblemen around him. He had no power himself, and bitterly resented it when a neighboring duke levied taxes on him.

"They're all talking about the latest tax levy," he said, "something to do with a war levy. It is either gold or personnel to fight. I personally prefer to send two men, rather than to deplete my monetary resources. This duke is preparing to battle the next kingdom, and I am completely annoyed and fed up with constant levies and useless conflicts." In this lifetime, he married for political reasons, and his relationship with his wife was unhappy. He died of old age, surrounded by his family, but feeling little warmth for anyone about his bedside.

In his ninth life, from 1590 to 1618, he was again a female. In this life, he lived in Wales. It was an unusual life in that the Welsh girl who he was had a romance with a Spanish seaman, who had apparently been shipwrecked near the shore where she lived, and became pregnant. The seaman disappeared and the girl suffered great shame for carrying an illegitimate child. She died in childbirth, full of bitterness and fear, sure that she would be condemned to hell for her sin. When I took Bob to the between-life experience after death as the Welsh girl, he explored the purpose of that lifetime and became aware that the Spanish sailor in the Welsh lifetime had also been the wife of the Egyptian cart driver in the earlier life.

In Bob's next lifetime, the tenth, he was once more a male, this time a French peasant who tended fields of millet and whose only possession was a wooden spoon that he treasured deeply. After Bob came out of hypnosis, he was amused at his deep pride in his wooden spoon and remarked, "When I think of all the worldly goods I have now, I think that that French peasant valued his spoon more than I value all the furnishings in my home."

In his eleventh lifetime, Bob was a prosperous English business-man who dealt in woolens, a successful merchant able to afford a home in a London square. He managed his business until he was around sixty-five and then turned it over to his son. His marriage was happy and he felt close to his wife and children. He seemed to enjoy his work, which took him to Scotland and France, both the buying of wool from peasants and distributing the woolen goods of his company. Since the span of this lifetime was from 1715 to 1790, I asked him if he was aware of the war with the Colonies. He responded angrily, "The colonies! Their cotton is hurting our wool business!"

Life number twelve was a shift in race again. Bob was a male in a lifetime from 1810 to 1870, and back in Egypt once more. When I tapped into the lifetime in 1860, he was supervising machin-ery in a cotton mill. Again he was involved with fabrics, but now the material was cotton, and his job was to work with new ma-chinery imported from England. The English woolen merchant succeeded by the Egyptian cotton-gin engineer represented an inter-esting transition. In this lifetime in Egypt, he had only one son, and his wife died young. He focused most of his attention on his work, and died of a heart attack at the age of sixty.

In Bob's thirteenth lifetime, he was a male again, born within four months of his death as an Egyptian engineer. This time he was an urchin who hung around the docks of London, England, evidently living by his wits, although in his earlier years he had been cared for by an old woman. When he was around eleven years old, the captain of an English ship called the *Dolphin* took him on board as a cabin boy. He developed a father-son relationship with this captain as they sailed around the world. Especially noteworthy in this lifetime was a stop the ship made in a South Sea island near New Zealand, where Bob, as a young cabin boy, became close to a native chieftain. Apparently, the captain of the *Dolphin* was very much interested in the myths and legends of the island natives, and the captain, the native chief, and the cabin boy spent several months together on the island. Interesting stories about the myths of these peoples came out of this recall, but of course there is no way to check their accuracy. All we were able to find out was that there was an English ship called the *Dolphin* under British registry in that time period.

Bob's fourteenth life was as a female who was born in 1900 and died in 1902 in Baltimore, Maryland. This was a death in early childhood, so after Bob experienced the death, which was again nontraumatic, as deaths in infancy seem to be in my samples, I asked him why he had died so young.

"I seemed to know after I'd been born that I'd chosen the wrong parents," he replied. "Apparently, I knew this wouldn't work out well, so I just left."

Bob's fifteenth life is as a male born in California in 1930. In this present lifetime he has utilized the skills of the merchant, the fabric dealer, and now, in his later years, some of the insights he felt he acquired in ancient Egypt.

Other than the interplay of vocational interests, it is hard to see a clear karmic pattern emerging from this panorama of fourteen past lives. Bob lived nine lives as a male and five as a female. He seemed to enjoy the male lives more than the female lives, but again there is a stretch of eight hundred years in which we have no past-life recall. He seemed to resist becoming aware of females lives, so it is possible he did not recall lives in this period because they were female. If so, a balance closer to fifty-fifty would have been achieved. Racially, he was Egyptian, Central American Indian, and Caucasian. He reported no lives in Asia.

We were able to check some of the material Bob gave us about the lifetimes in ancient Egypt. The hieroglyphics he drew while in the hypnotic state were analyzed by an Egyptologist, who reported that 80 percent of them were used in ancient Egyptian scripts, but the style of writing was that of someone who was drawing a picture he had seen rather than writing the way a scribe would have written. The Egyptian Bob spoke was more difficult to analyze. The Egyptologist said that 50 percent of the syllables were apparently used in Egyptian speech, but obviously we have no tape recordings of ancient Egyptian language, so this is only an estimate.

Some of the material on Bob's life as an English woolen merchant did check out, but in most of his other lifetimes, all that could be researched was the general appropriateness of his dress, living conditions, and climate in the places where he reported he had lived.

I could find no instances of errors or anachronisms in these fourteen lives. Bob is a well-educated subject who reads widely and is knowledgeable about history. He had no way of knowing Egyptian hieroglyphics except through having seen them in books. The results of our research were positive, but I felt that they were still not sufficient to prove that Bob had actually lived these lives.

Again, proving past lives was elusive. I wanted a method that would provide a large amount of data from many subjects. Only then could I rule out the effects of prior knowledge on the part of one subject. Could people who had never been hypnotized before give me the kind of material my subjects had reported? If ordinary people with no great interest in the subject could produce the same kinds of phenomena as Bob and Shirley, perhaps I could find the answers I was seeking.

6

THE MYSTERIES OF HYPNOSIS

It was necessary to rethink my research project. The phenomenon of past-life recall under hypnosis clearly existed, but how to relate it to the real world? It was like netting gorgeous sea creatures in the ocean of the subconscious. When I brought them to shore for examination, they seemed to dry up and scatter into fragments. Was I chasing rainbows?

I decided to begin at the beginning again. I had to describe in more detail the "ocean of the subconscious"—its currents, its colors, the rhythm of its waves; and I had to look carefully at the net I was casting to capture my "sea creatures": hypnosis. Exactly what was hypnosis?

Where in the brain did past-life recalls originate? Could I define the region of reincarnation memories more precisely than as "the subconscious?" Recent neurological research has led to a new concept of the brain's functioning: Briefly, the gray matter, or cortex, is divided into two separate halves connected by a band of nerve tissue called the corpus callosum. The left or dominant half is concerned with the "real world": language functions, recorded impressions from the world around us, and the set of beliefs we share with our social group. I think of the left brain as the home of the ego, or what we think of as our conscious self.

I visualize the ego as a little guy in a gray flannel suit and tight necktie. His job is to get you safely through your waking day, to make sure that you pay your electric bill and don't offend the boss. He keeps up a constant chatter, telling you to do this or that, and insisting that you pay attention to what's happening in the world around you. He takes occasional coffee breaks, like when you've driven down a familiar road, and realize when you arrive home that you have no memory of the trip. The ego has taken time out, figuring you can get home on automatic pilot. He's grateful when you finally retire for the night. He's got you in a safe place—your bedroom—where nothing is likely to happen to you. He pops up again in the morning, when you "wake down" from your wider experiences in the sleep state. He's the character who makes you look at the clock ("time" only exists in its usual sense when the ego is on the job) and nags you into getting out of bed and on your way to work. Jealous of the time you spend in your right brain, he likes to insist he's been around all the time. He hates to admit that his job isn't all there is to your experience, so he makes sure you forget your dreams. He's especially good at pretending he's never off the job. "I wasn't asleep, or not paying attention. I was just resting my eyes. I heard everything you said," he insists indignantly when you catch him at one of his coffee breaks, such as when you are wool-gathering, sleeping, or under hypnosis.

So while the ego sits up there around your speech center in the temporal and frontal lobes of your left brain, what part of you hangs out in the right brain? That's where dreams come from, and artistic inspiration, scientific imagination, nightmares, and the dreamy flow of listening to music. But most of all, the right brain experiences emotions—good and bad ones, excited ones and bored ones. That's the weather station of your head, where storm clouds of negative feeling swirl, and where sunny skies register, too. Skeins of cheerful music drift through the right brain and the clouds break up and the emotional weather is fine. The ego sends a message of impending danger across the corpus callosum bridge and the right brain responds with bursts of negative feeling. But who lives there?

We have a sense of self, of essential identity, when we dream, but it's not the old familiar ego. When we're in the right brain, we are ourselves as a small child; we are ourselves in another lifetime; we can be drops of rain as I was in my marvelous dream. We are a field of consciousness in our right brains, open to all the weathers and experiences and feelings that float through us.

Before I had hypnotized hundreds of people and watched them roaming the pastures of their right brains, I viewed this territory of the brain as a storage area. I visualized memories clicking into place in the forefront of consciousness, ordered up from the computerlike storage cells by my hypnotic instructions. But it doesn't seem to work like that. Instead, the right brain functions like an amplifier or tuner. I'd ask for an impression or image, and the right brain would search. Sometimes the impressions came in hazy and unfocused at first, until the right brain tuned them in sharply. Then competing images would fade away and one consistent set of images would flash into consciousness. Often, my subjects would sink deeper and the signal would fade into dreamlike symbolic images or fragments of the current lifetime. As the tuner drifted to signals far from earthly concerns, most of my subjects reported seeing vivid colors. This indicated to me that they were going into areas where the ego could not follow and they seemed to be "asleep." Maybe all the lifetimes ever experienced, all the feelings felt, are still out there in great waves in the universe. Maybe the right brain is an instrument for tuning into these waves, and not a storage area for memories.

One aspect of right brain functioning that I have found manifesting itself in every group I have hypnotized is the phenomenon of telepathy. I stumbled on this in my first group hypnosis when one subject reported that he found himself seeing the images just before he heard me ask the question. "But I've just done that," he said to himself. I question every group about this, and from 40 to 80 percent of the participants become aware that they are following my instructions before I give them. Apparently, they are so focused on the hypnotist that they follow my thoughts rather than my words. This is an awkward situation for me. I must monitor my thoughts carefully or I distort the results. One evening I was hypnotizing twenty people in my office. I took them to five time periods, including A.D. 25; and I flashed on a death I had experienced in a lifetime then. I had died of a heart attack, and leaving my body was difficult. When my subjects awoke, I found that twelve of the twenty had gone to A.D. 25 even though they had consciously wanted to go to other time periods. It's most unusual for that many subjects in any group to go to only one of the five time periods available to choose from, so I asked more questions. All twelve subjects in A.D. 25 and a few in other time periods reported that their hearts had been pounding uncomfortably through the first part of the hypnotic trip. I had never encountered this in a group before. All subjects reported a cessation of the strong heart thumping at roughly the same time in the trip, corresponding to the time when I pushed aside the image of the heart attack in A.D. 25. Seven of the twelve subjects in A.D. 25 then switched to lives in other time periods.

Telepathy among the members of the hypnotized groups also occurred, but it was much less frequent than telepathy between hypnotist and subject. This telepathy phenomenon helps me understand the strange things that often happen under the condition we call "hypnosis." Apparently, the ego agrees to relinquish temporary control of the "tuning knob" in the right brain. Normally, the right brain responds to commands from the left brain, the language-oriented ego. In most hypnotic states the subject's ego goes along on the trip, monitoring the experiences and judging whether or not to continue the experience. This circumstance led me to use a hypnotic technique in which I enlist the ego's cooperation and share control with the subject's left brain. The result, I believe, is that I am able to get 95 percent of my subjects relaxed and able to see images in the group hypnotic situation.

The group hypnotic technique is more effective than the one-to-one situation because the subject does not have to talk aloud. This relaxes some of the ego's fears that embarrassing things will be said, and allows for privacy of thought and experience. It also means that the left side of the brain, the speech centers, will not have to be activated and thus bring the subject out of the relaxed alpha and theta brain-wave states that produce the most vivid experiences.

I had begun choosing subjects for regression by interviewing subjects in groups. I had hypnotized the entire group all at once, asked questions under the hypnosis, and told my subjects not to speak until they awoke. Initially, I chose individual subjects for my research project who were unusually articulate, and who seemed to have vivid past recall. But I noticed that often up to 70 percent of my groups vividly recalled past-life experiences when they were hypnotized in the group situation. It grew harder to select the "best subjects" because all my subjects were getting past-life material.

Necessity became the mother of invention. I was on the faculty of a small university, and I had submitted my research proposals through the usual channels. I encountered the frustrating delays that most researchers run into when dealing with institutions. I was able to use university students as researchers, which was a big help, but there were costs involved, and it became increasingly obvious that the university would be unable to fund the hypnosis project and was increasingly doubtful about it. By this time I had a list of over a hundred fifty people who had heard of my research and wanted to be subjects, but no place on the university grounds to perform the regressions, no funds to support myself with while I was doing the research, and none of the usual facilities for typing transcripts and buying more recording equipment. Some of my would-be subjects suggested that I run a workshop. The humanistic psychology movement had evolved many ways for people to spend time exploring their inner consciousness, and they felt that exploring past lives was as good a way as any to move inward. I decided to charge a minimal fee for my workshop—thirty dollars for an eight-hour session with four hypnotic trips—and this would support my researches while I obtained the data I needed.

I planned my research as carefully as I could. I had done enough preliminary work to know what my hypnotic techniques should be. It was important, I discovered, to spend some time with my subjects before I took them under hypnosis. I explained to them what to expect when their eyes were closed, and tried to remove as much of the mystery from the process of hypnosis as I could. I found that subjects would go under hypnosis easily if they understood the process with their conscious minds. Attempts to bypass the ego, and to put subjects under hypnosis without their knowledge, seemed to me not only unethical, but unproductive.

In my group technique, the most important device for putting my subjects under hypnosis was to get them into rapid eye movement. I had learned that when I explained to them in advance that their eyelids would start twitching, and that some of them would want to open their eyes, more subjects would go under hypnosis. I only had to assure them this was a normal part of hypnosis and they were able to accept the experience and continue with it. When they were unwarned, however, the experience of twitching eyelids tended to wake them from the state.

Much of my hypnotic introductory patter is designed to get subjects into rapid eye movement. Sometimes this process is called fantasy imaging, sometimes guided fantasy, but it is the same whatever the name one gives it. I found that a technique developed by William Swygard was effective in getting my subjects to visualize with their eyes closed. In this technique, the subject is taken to his own front door and asked to see it clearly. Then he is taken in his imagination to the rooftop of the building where he lives, and asked to examine the surrounding territory. Next, he is told that he is lifting gently off the roof of his building and flying, as he has done in his dreams. At this point I introduced my subjects to the sensation of flying rapidly over the treetops to a favorite ocean beach. A guided fantasy followed, in which I had them soaring higher and higher into the air, seeing the curve of the earth at the horizon as they flew into the blue sky. Most of my subjects thoroughly enjoyed this sensation of soaring, and I let them savor it for several moments in the hypnotic induction.

I then provided them with a fluffy white cloud, and suggested that they stretch out on the cloud and relax further as I took them into past time periods. I had discovered that if I took subjects back directly to "the time before you were born," they would sometimes be drawn to upsetting past-life experiences. But if I gave them a choice of five different time periods and suggested that they choose one to experience that would not be distressing, very few had unpleasant experiences.

I had also discovered that at the end of the hypnotic trip it was important not only to restore energy so that they would awaken with a pleasant feeling, but also to suggest to them that any unpleasant emotional material would be soothed and would not disturb them after they awakened. To accomplish this, I evolved a guided fantasy trip at the end of the hypnotic session that seemed to have good results. I took my subjects back to the cloud after they had gone through the death experience in the past life. After relaxing them further to the count of five, I told them that there would be a tightly budded rose in their solar plexus. I told them that they were surrounded by a white light on their cloud, and that the rays of energy from the light would gently unfurl the petals of the rose until its heart was exposed. The white light would enter through the heart of the rose and suffuse their entire body with wave energies of peace and harmony, sealing over any unpleasant emotions. I chose the solar plexus as the location for this fantasy, based on the kundalini yoga concept of the solar plexus chakra as the seat of emotion.

When I brought my subjects out of hypnosis, I used a gradual, gentle method of returning them to the here-and-now. I told them they would see a golden ball of energy sparkling out in a far corner of space. "The ball of energy floats down through the darkness of space, penetrates the atmospheric envelope of earth, comes to the Western Hemisphere, comes down into this room, and enters the crown of your head. As the ball of energy enters the crown of your head, it brings health, vitality, and a sense of well-being to all the atoms and molecules, organs and organ systems of your body." I then slowly counted to ten and said, "Open your eyes. You are awake."

I had discovered that in the rapid-eye-movement state character-
izing the hypnosis, it was not only visual images that my subjects
reported. All their sensory equipment worked well under hypnosis,
and some of the most vivid impressions came to them through
hearing, touch, taste, and smell. I had observed that when animals
are in the state of rapid eye movement, their ears and nose twitch,
indicating that the impressions they are having are not just visual.
The same is true of the mammal called man. So I would include
in my hypnotic technique instructions to touch, to hear sounds,
to taste, to smell, and to have emotions.

The fact that my subjects were able to report feelings they had
had in the past life was probably the most significant aspect of
the hypnosis. When they experienced emotion in the past-life recall,
they tended to believe that it came from a deeper level than that
from which the visual images came. Perhaps I was exploring dreams,
but they were not merely the visual dreams that we so often report.

Now I had my technique for hypnosis, and I had a number of
subjects willing to try it. My next job was to lay out in advance
the kind of information I needed from my subjects, and to devise
my questions in such a way as to give me the information I required
to check theories.

I knew that the best way to check past-life recall was to relate
it to known historical reality. In individual cases, you check the
details in the time period and the place where the subject is reporting
the past life. So the object of my questions was to find out where
my subjects were, and in what time period. I discovered the time
period by asking my subjects to regress to each of five different
time periods. They then chose one of these time periods to explore
further. I found it was necessary to have an additional check on
the time in which they were living the past life, because many of
my subjects had images for time periods other than that to which
they had actually regressed. For that reason, I asked them after
they had died in that lifetime to flash on the year that they died
in modern terms. The dates usually flashed quite clearly, and corresponded well with the internal evidence my subjects reported during
the regression. When there was a conflict between the time period

they thought they had chosen and the date of death they flashed on, I found that the date flashed on was likely to be the valid one.

Figuring out where they were was more difficult. I did ask them to flash on the modern geographical name of the area after they had died, and many subjects did this. Still, there were often problems, so I set up a series of questions that would help locate my subjects, and would also serve as a check on the validity of their recall. I asked them to see the color of their skin, whether their hair was curly or straight and what its color was, and I asked them about the landscape and climate they found themselves in. My purpose was to see if they were of the appropriate race for the place they had chosen, and whether the landscape and climate corresponded to what we know of the area.

Next I wanted to get information of the kind I could check in archeological texts and historical records. I asked my subjects to visualize the food they were eating in the past life, because there are many records of the kinds of foodstuffs eaten in each time period and place. I also asked them to see the eating utensil and other household objects they were using, because this too could be checked.

The next series of questions related to commerce in the past-time period and place. I decided to ask my subjects to go to a market to get supplies and to describe the market and the supplies that they bought. Money is also a clue to a place and time in the past, so I asked them to visualize the money they might have exchanged for goods.

Other areas that could be checked were the architecture they saw and the kind of clothing and footgear they wore. Not only could I see whether the clothing they described was accurate according to historical texts, but I could tell whether other subjects in the same time period and in the same place wore similar types of clothing.

The death experience was also researched. Were the kinds of out-of-body experiences reported at death by Dr. Raymond Moody and Dr. Elisabeth Kubler-Ross also to be found in my subjects' deaths? I knew of Dr. Karlis Osis' work in exploring the death experience in our culture and in India, and I felt my research offered an interesting opportunity to get more material in this area. I told my subjects: "You will now go to the day you died. You will experience no pain and no fear, and if the experience is uncomfortable for you, you will return to your cloud and not experience it. Now it is the day of your death. Where are you? About how old are you? Now you will become aware of the cause of your death. Now death is very near. How do you feel about the prospect of dying now that it is so close? What have you been taught happens after death? Now the spirit is leaving the body. Allow yourself to experience the spirit leaving the body. What are you experiencing now?"

As you can see, my hypnotic instructions include the suggestion that the spirit will leave the body. My experience with subjects has been that recall of the death experience can sometimes be traumatic, and I was very careful to avoid such a development with my workshop subjects. I wanted to explore the feelings they had immediately after death in the past life. I was also curious about the cause of death. Would the subjects in my sample have natural deaths, or would they have experienced dramatic incidents of murder or suicide far beyond what could normally be expected? If there was an excess of violence in my sample, it would indicate to me that we were dealing with fantasy rather than an accurate recall of past life.

I also wanted to know how old my subjects were at the time they died, because in the past most people did not have life spans as long as those we enjoy today. Thus, this became one of the full set of questions regarding the death experience that I asked my subjects under hypnosis.

I decided to require that each subject experience three past-life recalls. There were several reasons for this. First, I wanted to check whether individual subjects tended to have the same type of past life in each of their regressions. If past-life recall is fantasy, one would expect the personality dynamics of the subject to be reflected in each of the past-life recalls he or she experiences. For example, a subject who showed a great deal of aggression in one past-life recall should show the same signs in two additional recalls.

I also needed at least two regressions to cover all of the time periods I wished to explore. Five time periods contained about as many images as my subjects could hold in their minds during the hypnotic trip; giving them ten periods to choose from would be to introduce too much confusion into the hypnotic instructions. I also wanted to check whether those time periods about which our culture is relatively well-informed with regard to clothing, social class, architecture, and historical events would result in more vivid past-life recall than information obtained when I took subjects to distant time periods for which we have little information.

So on the first trip I took my subjects to five time periods they might have known through reading a book or seeing a movie. Then, as a contrast, on the second trip I took them to time periods about which they were not likely to have information about life as it was lived. Would the first trip be more vivid? If past-life recall was fantasy, it should be more vivid in those time periods about which we have information that we can weave into our fantasies.

On the second trip I decided to ask questions about skills learned and about occupations. I would take my subjects to their childhood and ask them what skills they were learning. Again, I could check with information in historical texts, giving me additional opportunity to determine if the past-life recall were fantasy. I also decided to give my subjects some romantic experiences on the second trip, and asked them what their relationships were with the opposite sex at the age of seventeen.

I needed a third past-life hypnotic trip to check on whether my instructions regarding time periods were distorting my data. Instead of taking my subjects to a time period on the third past-life trip, I took them to geographical areas around the world. Would they choose different geographical areas if I suggested this rather than time periods? Would they all choose modern time periods if

I took them around the world, because they could know more about them in their conscious, waking life and thereby construct a better story under hypnosis?

So I set up trip three as a check on whether the results I was getting about time periods were being distorted by how I was asking my questions. I also wanted to know more about landscape and climate than my questions on trips one and two had provided, so in that life I would take my subjects on a journey and have them observe the scenery more closely. Since I also wanted to hear about religious observances in past time periods and places, on trip three I would ask them to go to a religious ceremony to see whether the religious observances they experienced in the past-life recall were appropriate for the time period and place they had chosen.

On all three trips, I explored information on costume, architecture, and climate. The death-experience questions were the same for all three past-life trips.

Another purpose of requiring three past-life trips from each subject was to determine if the material changed as the subject became more accustomed to hypnosis and went deeper into the hypnotic state with each trip. Would the information become more vivid?

I memorized my questions so that I would be sure to ask exactly the same questions in each workshop. I had found that to vary even one word of my hypnotic suggestions and questions changed the responses of my subjects; it was therefore important that I not deviate from the formula I had set up in advance. I prepared data sheets for each of the three trips, with the questions written out and spaces left for my subjects to write in the answers that came to them under hypnosis. Armed with my experience to date, I was ready to go, ready to start this exploration into past-life recall. What would I discover?

7

GATHERING THE DATA

The subjects arrived at my office in Walnut Creek, California, carrying their pillows and blankets and the sack lunch I had suggested they bring for our all-day hypnotic session. This was to be the fortieth group of subjects I had regressed; I was now nearing the end of my data-collecting goal. I had already examined the statistics from eight hundred data sheets and had written up the results in a magazine article. These results were so interesting that I decided to see if I could repeat my statistical survey on a new sample of subjects. It could be that the data that worked out so well might be the result of having an unusually knowledgeable group of subjects. I decided to hypnotize additional subjects until I had collected three hundred more data sheets, so that I could see whether my results would be the same with the second group as with the first.

It was important to repeat my findings; it is often easy enough to do a successful experiment, but more difficult when attempts are made to repeat it. I sent out the word that I was looking for more subjects, and twelve people had responded and come to this Saturday morning workshop. They were from all over the San Francisco Bay area; some of them had driven as much as a hundred miles to participate in the research.

The first to arrive were Jan, Frances, and Pat, three women who were friends and worked together in a large office. Pat had been hypnotized by her doctor when she gave birth, and had found that the hypnosis worked well for her. She had read of my work and called my office to ask if she and her friends could attend a workshop. Jan and Frances had never been hypnotized before, and though all were very interested in the topic of reincarnation, they had read little about it.

The next to come was Peter, who had driven down in an old VW from his home north of San Francisco. Peter, about thirty years old, was a dropout from the competitive society of cities. He was knowledgeable about spiritual matters and had taught yoga. Peter was the most sophisticated subject in this group.

Eleanor and John arrived next. They were a middle-aged couple who had long been interested in the field, but neither had been hypnotized prior to today's session. John had been through Werner Erhard's est training, so I knew he was likely to be a good subject. Many of the est "processes" are quite similar to experiences under hypnosis. Eleanor and John had heard of my work through a friend who had been in an earlier workshop.

Mike and Janet came in after Eleanor and John. They were a couple in their mid-twenties who had also been referred by friends who had had an interesting experience in an earlier workshop. The two people who referred them had found themselves in the same time period and place, and realized that they had known each other in a past lifetime. Both wrote down their experiences before talking with each other, thus confirming the evidence that they were in close communication with each other. Either they had been in that past life together, or their minds were so close that telepathic communications were picked up and they shared the same experience under hypnosis. Mike and Janet had never been hypnotized, and were not particularly interested in the occult. They just wanted to share the kind of experience their friends had had.

Next to arrive were Sherryl and Marilyn, who were social workers in their late twenties interested in using hypnosis as a therapeutic tool. Both used some guided fantasy techniques in their work, and wanted to see how my technique compared with those they had experienced before. Though they were interested in reincarnation, they were not "true believers."

Last to come were Jonathan and Lynn. Jonathan was a graduate student in physics at the University of California at Berkeley. One of his friends, a graduate student from Germany, had described my work enthusiastically. Johnathan was skeptical but curious. He had tried some biofeedback alpha training, and was intellectually knowledgeable about right- and left-brain research, but he had no acquaintance with the occult and was not a believer in reincarnation. His girlfriend, Lynn, was an undergraduate student at the University of California. She was very interested in all phenomena regarding past lives, and told me she thought that past-life recall must be true, because "it explains so many things about my life."

These twelve subjects—eight women and four men—were, I realized, typical of my entire subject population. Only one had been formally hypnotized in the past, though two were therapists themselves and one was an expert in yoga meditation. The remainder of the group had little background in altered states of consciousness and could be considered "naive" subjects.

Leona Lee, my associate, told them to spread their blankets and pillows out on the floor and make themselves at home. I become relaxed when I'm hypnotizing groups because I follow my own suggestions to relax; and if I lie down, I'm likely to go all the way under, and my poor subjects just have a good nap. So I sat in my hypnotizing chair, and my twelve subjects watched me intently. I understood their anxiety. What would they find out today? I began my introduction to the eight-hour hypnotic workshop:

"I know when you came today you thought to yourself, 'What if I can't be hypnotized? What if I didn't have a past life?' You won't have to worry about that. Ninety percent of my subjects go under hypnosis without difficulty, and flash on the answers to my questions while they're under. Your problem is not that you can't be hypnotized. Instead, you will find yourself struggling with the question, 'But did I make it all up?' The impressions are easy to get. What is difficult is to decide whether they are fantasy, coming from your own memories of books and movies, or whether they reflect a past reality. You'll find yourself struggling with this question for some time."

The group relaxed a little as my introduction continued. I explained about the rapid eye movements that they would probably experience, and told them that their subconscious would have control over their experience of the past-life recall. I assured them that in the instructions regarding the past-life death, they would be told to move away from the death experience if they were feeling any discomfort. Several of them looked relieved when they heard me say this, so I realized this was one of the reasons they felt anxious about the hypnosis.

I went on to explain to them that they would be exploring their own sleep states: "You'll find that you're going to understand more about your own mind at the end of this workshop. Whether past-life recall is fantasy or reflects reincarnation, you're going to experience some interesting places in your own mind. I want your ego to go along on the trip. If there is no involvement of your conscious self in the hypnosis, you'll be unable to remember your experiences and you won't be able to fill out the data sheets for me. So keep your ego along on the trip and let it chatter away to you. But at the same time, try to let images, feelings, thoughts, and impressions come up from your subconscious into your conscious mind in response to my questions and suggestions."

I told them all to stretch out on the floor, suggesting they kick off their shoes and make themselves as comfortable as they could. "It's like going to sleep at night," I explained. Then I told them to yawn, and I began the hypnotic induction. As I went through the guided-fantasy portion of the trip, I checked and saw that most of them were having rapid eye movements. I continued to relax them, and then took them back through five time periods in the past. "When I call out a time period, let an image come into your mind," I said. I called out the time periods—1850, 1700, 1500, A.D. 25, and 500 B.C. Then I asked them to choose one of these time periods to explore further and instructed them to allow their subconscious to choose a time period that would not be upsetting to them. My voice droned on as I took them through the same questions I had asked many times before in hypnotic sessions. I felt my own mind drifting as I heard my voice repeat the familiar questions.

There are times when I feel that I am hearing my own voice off in the distance, and when I get this feeling, I open my eyes and return to the room so that I don't drift too far from my subjects. At the same time I am asking the questions aloud, I am also concentrating intently on my subjects. I try to send thoughts of comfort and good will toward them so they will feel at ease while they are under hypnosis. I do this automatically, without rationalizing it to myself. I don't get mental impressions of images my subjects are experiencing—at least I haven't noticed any—but I do seem to be aware if anyone is experiencing any physical or emotional difficulty, and I then interject suggestions that they will feel no pain and that any disturbance will be soothed away. This doesn't happen often under hypnosis, but when it does, I find it interesting that I receive these flashes telepathically. After the subjects awaken from hypnosis, they often confirm my feeling that they were experiencing something unpleasant at the moment I was sending them reassuring thoughts; and they say the hypnotic suggestion to relax did indeed help them.

Today no one seemed to be in any difficulty, and the hypnotic session went smoothly. I brought my subjects to the death experience, and then took them back to their cloud. When I gave the suggestion of the tightly budded rose in the solar plexus, I saw a look of deep peace and pleasure come over Peter's face. His eyes were still closed and he still appeared hypnotized, but the experience of the rose opening and the ball of light seemed to be affecting him.

I gave all the subjects the posthypnotic suggestion that they would remember vividly what they experienced, and that they would fill out their data sheets easily upon awakening. I concluded the hypnosis by saying, "You will not share your experience with others until you have completed your data sheet. Then you will feel comfortable in discussing your experience with the others in the group."

At the count of ten, I brought them out of hypnosis, and saw the phenomenon of their opening their eyes simultaneously. Like all my subjects in past sessions, they seemed extremely relaxed, and it took them a few moments to sit up and become physically active again. I passed out the data sheets for trip one and gave each person a pen. I explained that I was going to go out of the room for ten minutes to relax while they filled out their forms.

When I came back into the room, they were still writing busily. I noticed that Eleanor had not filled out her sheet. Soon they had finished, and I came to the part of the workshop I like the best. I am always very curious as to what has happened as a result of the questions I asked under hypnosis. A part of me is still surprised that so many people come up with past-life recalls, even though that is what I am suggesting under the hypnosis. And what a diversity of experiences my subjects have!

But first, before I heard their stories, I needed to ask them two questions to determine whether they had been hypnotized. "How long did it seem to you, in minutes, from the time I said, 'Close your eyes,' to the time I said, 'Open your eyes'?" I asked the group. Guesses came thick and fast; four people guessed fifteen minutes, five guessed twenty minutes, one guessed half an hour. The other two said that they really couldn't estimate, "because it seemed like no time at all and yet it also seemed like hours."

I told them, "It was fifty minutes. You lay on the hard floor without moving for nearly an hour."

They were surprised at this; they were sure it hadn't been that long. I pointed to the clock on the wall, and the evidence of their own eyes convinced them. For reasons I don't understand, my subjects under hypnosis commonly believe that they have been under for only fifteen or twenty minutes. Just as time seems to lengthen when people are stoned on marijuana, so it appears to contract when they are under hypnosis. Eleanor was one of the people who didn't hazard a guess about the time. I asked her, "How long did it seem to you?"

"Well, it seemed like forever. My back was hurting, and I could hear the breathing around me. I just couldn't seem to get any images. I would try, but then you seemed to go so fast that just as I was starting to think of something, you moved on. I was really anxious for you to wake us up so I could stretch and relieve my painful back."

"You were the subject who was not hypnotized," I told her. "If you thought it was a long time and if you were intensely aware of physical discomfort the whole time, there's no doubt in my mind that you were not hypnotized. Next time try the sofa over there. It might make you more comfortable, and that will help to get you under."

I then asked the question that always intrigues me. "Were any of you a little bit ahead of me on this trip?" Seven of the twelve subjects raised their hands. Peter said, "I was ahead of you the whole time. It seemed that I knew what you were going to say before you said it. I didn't notice it until about halfway through the trip; then I decided to ignore it and just move with you."

Marilyn reported, "You know, I didn't realize that I was doing that until you asked me. Then I remembered. I was ahead of you at least three or four times on the trip. I thought I wasn't following instructions right."

I explained to the group that this phenomenon of answering my questions before I articulate them was present in every group that I had hypnotized. Apparently, when one is functioning in the right brain and is in the rapid-eye-movement state, telepathic communication is more usual than hearing words. This is such a fascinating phenomenon that I am now conducting extensive research on telepathy under hypnosis with groups in which I give some of my instructions verbally and others only telepathically.

I asked the group members about their experiences under hypnosis. "How many of you went to the time period 1850?"

Jan responded that she had been in Kansas in that period. "Many of my images were dim. It seems as though I was straining to get answers to your questions. I did feel the material of my dress, and found that it was a rough weave, kind of a homespun, but I couldn't get clear images of my hands or the place where I was living. When you asked us to see who was eating a meal with us, I got a flashing image of a tall, dark-haired man with a beard. I felt kind of apprehensive about him. When you asked about the death, I found myself back on a cloud and I didn't really experience it."

I explained to Jan that many subjects—about 15 percent—often have rather dim images at the beginning of the hypnotic sessions. "Did you feel as though you were making this up from things you had read?" I asked her.

"Yes, I did," Jan responded. "I wrote down at the bottom of my form, where you have "Additional Comments," that I felt I was making it all up. Except for the feel of my dress, it did seem to be forced."

John broke in, "My trip in 1850 was very vivid. I don't know why, but everything just flashed into my mind with colors and detail. In some of it I seem to be seeing things, but I also smelled the smells at the marketplace, and heard voices around me during the exciting event. I seem to start out in that lifetime in England, but went to South Africa and died there in 1898. When you took me to the death experience, I was old. I must have had a fever because I was aware of being very hot. When I died, I seemed to float up from my body and look down at the body below me. I had a deep feeling of release and joy at death. The experience was so intense that tears ran down my cheeks. I mean right here and now, tears ran down my cheeks. That was some vivid trip!"

I explained to the others that the kind of trip John experienced was at least as common as the more vague hypnotic experience Jan had described. "Some subjects seem to get this immediately, and go through the experience with full involvement," I told them. "Others slip into the experience gradually and it takes several hypnotic sessions to reach this level."

Marilyn then described her trip in the 1850s: "But it seemed closer to the 1900s. The dresses looked like 1910 or so. I saw myself in New York. At least it was a city with quite tall buildings and very crowded streets. But I felt myself drifting off, and by the time you took me to the death experience, apparently I fell asleep, because I don't remember anything else until you told us to open our eyes."

This also happens to some of my subjects: They go under too deep to recall any of the material occurring under hypnosis. It is rare on the first hypnotic trip, but occurs increasingly as the trips continue.

"Was anyone living in the 1700s?" I asked.

Frances and Sherryl both said they had been alive in that time period. Frances reported that she had found to her great surprise that the boots she was wearing were obviously masculine. "Then, when I looked at my clothes and my hands, I realized that I was a man. I seemed to be some kind of laborer, because there was mud on my boots and my clothing was rough. My hands were calloused and work-worn. I was standing in a plowed field, but could see a small hut in the distance. Apparently, this was where I lived, because I found myself eating my evening meal in this small dark hut. I ate with a wooden spoon from a wooden bowl, and around me were my wife and three children. I didn't seem to have a warm feeling towards my wife, but my oldest son was next to me and I felt much love for him. When you took me to the death, it was some kind of accident with horses. All I know is that it happened very fast, and I was out of my body before I seemed to know what had happened.

"The main experience at death was one of great surprise to find myself outside my body. Then I had a feeling of lightness and I was glad that that lifetime was over. It was a hard-working life. The date of my death flashed as 1721, and the place where I lived was around Arles, France."

Sherryl reported, "I was a woman. I was wearing a long rough-textured dress with an apron over it and a kind of white cap with wings on each side. I couldn't figure out at first what the cap was, and thought maybe I was a nun, but I seemed to be working in some kind of marketplace selling produce. When you asked about the evening meal, I was sitting by myself in a small, dark place. No one seemed to be around me, but I had the impression that there was a man who usually sat on my right and that he wasn't there that evening. When you asked about the exciting event, all I could see was a crowd of people in the marketplace, and heard a great deal of shouting. It seemed as though people were frightened or angry. That's all I could get.

"When you took me to my death, I was back in the hut lying on straw. I seemed to be dying of old age, or at any rate I couldn't sense any particular reason for my death. It was a very gentle and easy death, and when I floated out of my body, I thought that I had done well in that lifetime. I don't know why I had that feeling. Death was the best part of the trip for me. After I saw my body, I was soaring higher and higher into the sky and I left the body with no regrets."

Lynn also had been a male, but in the 1500s. "When I looked down at my feet I saw some kind of sandal, a wooden sandal," she said. "I was wearing a short-pant outfit with an overblouse. My hair was straight and black and my hands were slightly tan in color. It was when I looked at the landscape and saw buildings I realized I was in Japan. I seemed to be living in some small fishing village, and the exciting event was a storm when I was out on a boat. This also turned out to be where I died, because apparently I fell overboard or the boat was overturned during a storm. But I can remember most vividly the countryside we could see from our boat as we went out of the harbor. It was so beautiful and serene.

"My experience after death was that I felt shocked at what had happened, and was confused at first. Then I could not see my body, I guess because it was under water. But it seemed to me that after I died I was joined by the two others who had been on the boat with me. This is only a fleeting impression."

Peter reported that he had been in A.D. 25. "Frances said that she was surprised to find herself a man," he remarked. "I was surprised and a little upset to find that I was a woman. I was wearing some kind of gauzy draped garment which looked like an Indian sari. When you asked to see a building, I could see a large ceremonial building that looked like pictures I've seen of an Indian temple. The food I ate was some kind of flat bread and a mixture of vegetables. It tasted very spicy. I ate with my fingers from a roughly carved wooden bowl. At first I couldn't tell what the exciting event was, but I think it was my marriage. I know I felt apprehensive and excited at the same time. I could hear bells at the ceremony. When you took us to the evening meal, apparently it was before I was married. I could see my father and two sisters eating with me.

"At the death, I flashed that I was dying in childbirth. Though you told us we would feel no pain, I felt the oddest kind of sensation in the pelvic region. Of course, I have no idea what it's like to have a baby." Peter laughed, and the rest of us joined in. "There was a kind of pulling sensation in the pelvis and then I seemed to be rather feverish. I don't know exactly when I left my body; it was as though I was going in and out of the body for some time. Then I was out of the body and I saw the most gorgeous colors around me. It was a very beautiful experience, the death. But even while I was enjoying the beautiful colors, I felt a deep sense of regret at leaving behind two other children that I had."

I commented to the group that death in childbirth appeared to be the most difficult of all the deaths in my sample. The problem seemed to be a regret at leaving children who are dependent, rather than sorrow at the death itself.

Janet told us that she had been a male in A.D. 25. "The map was somewhere in northern Italy around the Adriatic Sea. I lived in a stone village. The houses were quite clear to me. They were one-story, with low doorways. I seemed to be working with wood. I guess I was a carpenter. When I went to the marketplace, I bought grain and some kind of tool that I must have used in my woodworking business." She described the tool to us, and it was one reported by another subject, who also had had a life in Italy in that same time period. It appeared to be a primitive kind of saw.

Janet continued, "I ate with other men at the table. They didn't seem to be related to me; it was as though somehow we all worked together or lived together. I had the feeling that my family was somewhere in the countryside and that I worked in this village. The coin I used to buy my supplies was interesting. Actually, I had two coins. One of them was a dull gold color, and it had the raised head of what looked like an emperor or something on it. The other coin was a dark gray and had a hole in the middle. It seemed to be shaped like a square with the corners pounded to try to make it look round. I've never seen anything like it!"

I broke in, "I've had that coin described to me at least twenty times before. It was used around the Mediterranean Sea in the time period 500 B.C. to A.D. 25. Did it seem to be crude around the edges?" I asked.

Janet replied, "Yes, as though it had been hammered rather than molded. When you took me to the death experience," Janet went on, "I seemed to be in my fifties. But just as I started to experience the cause of death, I found myself back on the cloud. I didn't experience anything again until you said that we had left the body. Then I saw my body lying on a bed of straw. It looked as though there had been some damage to the head. I really don't know what caused my death. But leaving my body was very pleasant."

Three of the group were in 500 B.C. Jonathan reported that he had been a man in that time period and that he had lived in a city in the Middle East. He spoke about what he saw: "There were gardens around, but they seemed to be about one floor above me. I was walking between stone walls of one-story construction. There was greenery above me. You know, when Janet was describing her coin, I saw one much like that. It seemed to be six-sided, though I couldn't tell exactly. But it did have a hole in the middle. I bought food at the marketplace and there were open stalls with some kind of covering over the top like a tent. It was very crowded at the marketplace and I could smell many smells, including that of donkey dung."

Jonathan went on to describe his death of old age. He had a

very peaceful and contented feeling as he floated up from his body.

Mike spoke up next. "Well, I'm a little like Peter. I was shocked to find that I was a woman. But I seemed to be in China—at least that's where the map flashed after I died. The date of my death came flashing in as 482 B.C. It was a very peaceful life and I seemed to live in comfortable surroundings. My activities were largely cooking and caring for a modest home."

Pat joined the conversation, saying she had also been a woman in 500 B.C. "But my images were more like Jan's," she said. "I felt very lonely because every time I looked for someone else in that lifetime, I couldn't see faces. I seemed to be very much by myself. It was a primitive life and I was wearing rough hides around my body. All I remember was a campfire and roasting some kind of small animal that tasted greasy. I died in an accident of some kind. I fell off a cliff as I was walking down a rocky path. As I was tumbling in the air, I felt as though I went in two directions— my body fell to the rocks below, but I continued to float up. When you asked the geographical location, I saw a map with Central Asia pinpointed. I didn't flash on the date of death."

"Let's get going right now on the second trip," I told my subjects. I was planning to take them deeper into hypnosis this time, especially because Eleanor had not experienced hypnosis the first time. I have developed a special technique that I call, in less than scientific language, my "super zap." I would try it on the induction for this trip to see what the results would be with Eleanor. The technique consisted of taking my subjects to their childhood living room, getting them to recall vividly the furniture and surroundings they knew at the age of five, and then moving them to their childhood bedroom and to an out-of-body trip.

"Now you are lying in your bed," I said. "You are five years old. You are asleep and you're dreaming, yet you hear my voice, and it is easy for you to follow my instructions. You are sleeping in your bed. You are five. Now you are going to experience something that you knew when you were five. You are not going to sleep. You are going to become aware of a sensation of rising energy all around you. For some of you it may be a spinning sensation, and you're going faster and faster, though you're not dizzy. For others of you it's a feeling of expansion, as though you were growing larger and larger. There is a vibration of energy increasing all around you. The energy comes to a climax, and now you are floating out of your body. You are out of your body now, and you are floating out through the window of your childhood bedroom. You are free! Remember, now, your childhood dreams of flying."

After giving my subjects this suggestion, I emphasized that they would hear my voice and that they would come awake at the sound of my voice. But first I took them on a trip to time periods ranging from 2000 B.C. and 1000 B.C. to A.D. 400, A.D. 800, and A.D. 1200. I wanted to find out: Would the lives experienced in these obscure time periods be as vivid as the ones in known historical periods?

I awakened the subjects slowly from the second trip, and they opened their eyes slowly this time, lying still for a few moments, then looking around them. When I handed out the data sheets, they were slow to reach for their pens and begin the process of writing down their experiences. I had begun to recognize the expressions my subjects have after experiencing different states of hypnosis; it was obvious that this group had had a good time on the second trip and had been taken far from normal waking consciousness.

When they had finished writing down their experiences, I suggested that we talk about their trip while we ate our sandwich lunches. The group was still somewhat dreamy and relaxed as the result of the long hypnotic session, and there was an atmosphere of friendliness. If I sense any tension in a group composed of people who don't know each other, I give the posthypnotic suggestion on the first trip that they will feel comfortable in the group, and this has a decided effect. People relax markedly, the discussion of their experiences is lively, and all join in.

Jan told about her trip in A.D. 1200. She had been a man, and this time her trip was vivid, as opposed to the first regression, in which her images had been dim and unconvincing. "I saw colors this time, and I heard voices speaking in some language I couldn't entirely understand. I seemed to know what they were talking about, but it wasn't a direct translation of the language I was hearing. It was more that I just 'knew' what they were saying. I was some kind of a farmer—at least, in my mature life. When I was seventeen, I wanted to be a soldier. I don't know whether I ever fought in any battles, but in my adult life I found myself farming a plot of land, I died of old age, with my family around me. It was a most pleasant death this time. The map flashed as central Europe somewhere, and the year of my death was 1271.''

John said that he had some strange and interesting sensations on this trip. "When you took me to the childhood bed, I lost your voice for a while. I don't know where I went, but I know that something was going on. I didn't want to leave where I was to go on the past-life trip with you, but I did flash on an image of a mosque in the year 1200. I found myself wearing some kind of pantaloon trousers, walking down the streets of a fairly large city; I think it was Constantinople. But right after that, I seemed to leave the past-life trip and go back to wherever I had been when you took me flying out of my window in childhood. I heard your voice bringing me back when you were counting for us to awaken. I feel very relaxed now, but I keep wondering what it was that I experienced that I can't remember now.''

Peter reported that he had been in Italy in A.D. 800. "I think it was northern Italy, because I saw some high mountains in the distance. I was working with a pitchfork in a countryside setting. I was short and stout, with stubby little hands. I died fairly young, but I didn't know the cause. I think it was some kind of disease. Dying was strange. I seemed to leave my body through the top of my head, and I floated over this small dark hut, where my body lay. I had a sense of confusion. Then, just as I began to see a light, you took us out of the experience.''

Frances also had a vivid trip this time, as a woman somewhere in Asia. At first "the death scene was hard for me to understand,'' she said. "When you brought us to the death I felt a choking sensation in my throat, but then you said we would feel no pain and the feeling went away. But I can still sense it now," and she put her hand to her throat. "Apparently, there had been a flood, because after I left my body I saw it floating in an area with trees and other objects floating around it. I think something struck me in the throat as I fell into the water. Before the death, the life seemed rather ordinary. My childhood was happy, but in my mature life I was aware of being hungry."

None of the subjects had chosen A.D. 400 in which to experience a lifetime, but three of them had gone to 1000 B.C. Sherryl had been a male scribe in Egypt and at age eleven learned the skill of writing Egyptian hieroglyphics. She said she worked out in an open courtyard area rather than indoors. She could remember vividly her hand moving and shaping the hieroglyphics, but she wasn't able to copy them on her data sheet after she awoke. She died a natural death at a fairly young age.

Janet had been a woman in Asia, living with a primitive tribe in a mountainous area. Her home was a kind of dugout on the side of a hill. In her mature life, she found herself scraping hides. She died in childbirth. "I certainly was glad to leave that lifetime," she said. "I can smell the hides even now—not a very pleasant odor. I would have thought primitive life would be fun, but that life was hard. I was very glad to die and leave it."

Lynn had also been a woman, and also in Asia, but she lived on a flat plain near the sea: "There were a lot of buildings where I lived. They were flat-roofed and made of some sort of mud construction, like bricks. In my mature life I mostly seemed to cook some sort of grain and take care of my family. I died of old age."

Both Marilyn and Jonathan went to the year 2000 B.C. Marilyn said she flashed that she was in India, in an area near the Indus River. "It was a village. I was a man and I seemed to spend a lot of time talking with the other villagers. I don't know quite what it was I was discussing, but I seemed to be a leader of some kind. At least I didn't do any manual work when you took us to a day in our mature life. I was surprised to find I was wearing a rather finely woven garment. I wonder if they had looms in 2000 B.C.?"

Jonathan was a man in Mesopotamia. "It was a rather opulent society, as far as I could see. Although I was dressed in a rough woolen robe, I did see others in the village wearing decorated fabrics, and I did see jewelry. As a matter of fact, in my mature life I seemed to be working some kind of metal into a decorative object. I died through some kind of accident. It began suddenly, even before you took us to the death experience. I felt fear and apprehension. Then I felt something strike me in the midsection. Then it's all blank until you woke us up. I guess I just skipped the death."

Eleanor, Mike, and Pat all reported rather sheepishly that they didn't remember a thing from the time I told them to go to their childhood bed until I said, "Open your eyes, you're awake."

Eleanor was quite surprised at this experience. "I was afraid nothing would happen this time, like last time, but I decided not to worry about it and just relax. The next thing I knew, you were counting and asking us to open our eyes. I guess I really got hypnotized this time, but I still didn't have a past-life trip!"

Mike and Pat both said that they had seen their childhood living room in vivid detail. Mike said, "I'm going to ask my mother if we really did have draperies like that when I was five years old. I know I haven't thought consciously about the decoration of our living room for at least twenty years."

I explained to the group that I inserted the questions regarding their childhood living room because I wanted them to have something they could go back and check. "A past-life recall is often frustrating because you can't usually get any feedback on whether the images you saw were accurate," I said. "But if you did remember your living room vividly under hypnosis, you can check with members of your family to see if your recollections were correct. Such a memory is an example of 'cryptoamnesia,' of recalling details once known but long since consciously forgotten."

It was time for trip three. The group members stretched and relaxed and settled back on their blankets and pillows. I warned them, "This is after-lunch naptime. This time you will hear my voice telling you to stay awake. I find that it is increasingly difficult to keep my subjects in a light trance on the third hypnotic trip. So don't be surprised if I get rather bossy under the hypnosis and keep telling you to focus on my voice."

I began the induction quickly this time, knowing that all twelve members of this group could be hypnotized, so I didn't need a long induction procedure. I still gave them the experience of recalling something from the immediate past in their present life, for checking purposes. On the third trip, I suggest my subjects recall a vacation they've taken within the last five years, and get them to see vividly where they slept on the trip, and the scenery and people they saw. I then move them up into the sky and onto their fluffy white clouds.

"Now, you're going to float around the world," I said. "When I call out a place, let an image come into your mind."

As my instructions took them around the world to each continent, I asked them to choose a place to experience past life where the images were vivid, a place toward which they felt emotionally drawn. This instruction resulted in the most vivid trips of all. For my subjects, trip one is often the most exciting, probably because it is their first experience, but trip three often results in the most vivid emotions, because they are then in a deeper state of hypnosis. Also, they seem to have a wider range of past lives to dip into on the third trip because of the geographical instructions.

I asked them questions under hypnosis about a community event in that lifetime, about the language they heard spoken, about a journey they took, and about a religious ceremony. At the death experience on trip three, I again asked them to see how their body was disposed of. As the trip ended, I asked them if they had known anyone in that lifetime whom they know in their current lifetime. Many subjects are interested in finding out from their subconscious if they have shared past lives with people who are important to them now, so this question gives them an opportunity to explore such a possibility.

On this trip, I gave my subjects the posthypnotic suggestion that they would feel remarkably cheerful when they awoke, and when I brought them back to the here-and-now and woke them up, most of them awakened with a smile, and talked with one another even before the data sheets had been filled out. My instructions to be cheerful had certainly worked!

As had been the case with my other groups, trip three was the most impressive one for most of the subjects. Jonathan described a very strong feeling of love he had had during the religious ceremony, in which he had experienced marrying a childhood sweetheart.

"I know who she is now," he said. "A chill went through me when you asked if I knew anyone in that lifetime that I know today, and it flashed in my mind without doubt or question."

Eleanor had finally had a past-life trip: "I started to drift too deep, but then I heard your voice saying that I would wake up and go on the trip with you. I did, and it was amazing! I heard drums, and I first thought the drums were here in this room. Then I realized that I was in Africa. I was a man, and I was a hunter. It was a most happy life and I enjoyed it thoroughly. The religious ceremony had a lot of drums and chanting, but I don't know what it was we were celebrating. In my here-and-now body, I really felt that I was dancing. I was killed by some animal, but it wasn't as frightening as I thought it might be. It somehow seemed very natural that I should die this way and I felt no resentment toward the animal for killing me. There was much commotion in the village when the other hunters brought my body back, and I felt grateful to these people for caring that much about me."

My subjects were now comfortable with each other, and spent some time sharing their experiences. Lynn commented, "You know, I like doing this in a group. When I have these past-life experiences under hypnosis, part of my mind wonders why I'm coming up with all this. Somehow it makes it easier when I know that everyone else is having their own experiences, and that when it's over, we're able to talk them over with each other." She laughed. "It gets to seem almost normal to have past-life recall."

After they had shared their feelings and some of their ideas about the karmic connections they had noted in their trips, I sent them back to their blankets and pillows for the fourth hypnotic session. "Now I'm going to take you to the state between lives," I said, "to the time before you were born. In order to get this information, I need to take you to quite a deep level."

The results of the fourth trip, which are fascinating indeed, are the subject of continuing research and a forthcoming book.

When it was time to leave the workshop, they all gathered up their blankets and pillows and thanked me for the experiences they had had. "This has been a really fascinating day," Jonathan said. "I still don't know whether to believe it all, but there are some things I can look up to verify. At any rate, I learned more about myself today."

Peter lingered after the rest had left. "I've been studying Eastern mysticism for seven years now. I've experienced some deep states in meditation, and I've been comparing it with what I experienced in the hypnosis. There are some similarities, but I seem to feel more emotion under the hypnosis." He smiled and said, "The rose in the solar plexus was a powerful emotional experience for me. I found tears running down my cheeks—tears of joy—when you said this, and a rush of emotion came to me. This is a powerful state, hypnosis. I think I'll explore it further."

After Peter left, I gathered together the data sheets and began to evaluate the statistical information on social class, sex, geographical location, and other variables. As I entered the information from the data sheets into my data-collection ledgers, I realized that statistics can tell only a tiny part of the story. What effect would this workshop have on the lives of the people who came here to be subjects today? How could I ever measure the emotional responses they had? But what I could write down, collect, and arrange in charts and graphs were the data they had written on their sheets.

Feeling and emotion belong in a different world than numbers and graphs. Perhaps we need both in order to grasp as fully as possible the world around us, and to move closer to an understanding of the mysteries of being alive.

My data ledgers were almost complete now. I was ready to look at the "hard facts" and see what kind of answers emerged. Would the data support the idea that past-life recall was fantasy, or would they show a picture of life as it was actually lived in the past?

8

ADDING IT UP

After I collected the data sheets from my subjects at the end of each workshop, I went over each story to check for inaccuracies. I reasoned that if past-life recall were fantasy, my subjects would include material in their regressions that I could prove could not have been true. They might have seen anachronisms of one kind or another—clothing and architecture that was completely wrong for the time period and place they had chosen—or a climate and landscape that would not match the map they flashed on. So the first step in analyzing the data was to look for clear-cut discrepancies in the reported past lives.

To my surprise, I found only 11 data sheets out of the 1,088 I had collected that showed clear evidence of discrepancies. True, many of the lives reported were very humble, so the clothing was bound to be a rough tunic and the architecture a crude hut. These I could clearly neither prove nor disprove, and even where there were specific details, tracking them down posed problems. The reference books I used often described the architecture of the rich in each time period, but there was little in the literature about more humble dwellings, especially in the earliest time periods. I consulted books on costume, and again found that when there was specific information it was often only on the clothing worn by the wealthy. Only in those cultures in which drawings were made that have lasted through the centuries could I find any real details of costume.

An example of some of my problems in checking can be seen by looking at a collection of five data sheets describing lives in 2000 B.C. to 1000 B.C. in a region around the Caucasus Mountains in what is now Russia. This area was described by the subjects as mountainous and barren. Their maps showed the region north of Iran over toward Pakistan. In researching this area in those early time periods, I was not able to gain much information about the type of architecture. My subjects were apparently nomadic, and described tents and lean-tos rather than buildings. However, all five expressed surprise when they looked down at their hands and found that their skin was white. Three described their hair as light brown, and two as blond. Three of the subjects had written on their data sheets, "This doesn't seem right to me. I was surprised when the map flashed on Asia in the central area near the Near East. I think I should have had tan skin and dark hair."

All five subjects described themselves as wearing some kind of leather pants. Trousers were unusual in the regressions in the earliest time periods; only in this region did my subjects see themselves wearing pants. I researched the costumes worn at that time, and found an illustration of Scythians and Parthians clad in leather trousers. Furthermore, the population of this region was made up of the original Caucasians, and did have white skin and fair hair. So in these instances in which my subjects felt that their data were wrong, according to their own view of history, research showed that their unconscious had presented them with a more accurate picture of life in the Caucasus Mountains in 2000 B.C. than their conscious awareness.

This was to happen again and again as I checked the data on individual cases, and to me, it was the most evidential of all the material I collected in my research. If past-life recall is fantasy, one would expect our conscious knowledge of history to provide the images. When the images contrast with what we believe to be true, and yet prove on careful study to be accurate, then we must look anew at the concept of past-life recall as fantasy.

Of the eleven data sheets that provided evidence that the experience did not correspond with known past reality, it was primarily the mention of a particular object or historical event that proved to be false in terms of the time period chosen. For example, one subject reported playing a piano in the 1500s, when in fact the piano was not developed as a musical instrument until the 1700s. I therefore placed that data sheet in the file marked "Inaccuracies." Another data sheet went into the same file because the subject reported "teaching the code of Hammurabi" in 1700 B.C. Reference books reported that the code of Hammurabi was not developed until 1300 B.C. The other nine sheets contained similar inaccuracies, though I noted that the time periods were not very far off from the event described. It could be that in these cases my subjects' awareness of the time period was in error, rather than the past-life recall. But the data sheet went into the Inaccuracies file if *any* discrepancy was discovered. Altogether, my Inaccuracies file contained just under 1 percent of all the data sheets collected, a remarkably low figure.

Other data sheets had to be put into a file folder labeled "Went Too Deep." These were data sheets on which only the initial questions were answered, after which the subject might write, "After I saw the clothes I was wearing, I seemed to drift off. I got images of things like streetcars and the freeway, and before I knew it I seemed to fall asleep. I only awoke when you brought the ball of light down." There was a tendency for dreamlike images to occur at the point of transition from the past-life recall into the deeper state. I could have considered these reports inaccuracies, but did not because a clear pattern emerged. The past-life recall was begun, and the mind then drifted into other spaces and disconnected images appeared. Only a few subjects stayed aware enough under these circumstances to be able to fill out the data sheet.

As the hypnotic trips progressed in the workshops, more and more of my data sheets had scribbled on them this kind of report: "I lost you when you were going around the world. I don't know what I was experiencing because I can't remember now. But I know it felt good wherever I was, and I felt a reluctance to go into a past life."

The following pages discuss the topics covered in the data sheets more fully, and present my findings in tabular form so that the reader can see on the charts, for each time period, the distribution of social class, race, sex, and population; the types of clothing, footwear, and plates that were used; and the kind of death and emotion felt at the death experience.

Social Class in Past Time Periods

I was curious to know how many of my subjects had been wealthy or famous in a past life. A frequent objection to past-life recall is that so many people seemed to have been Cleopatra or high priests in Egypt in past lives. Would that also be true of my large sample of more than a thousand cases? I analyzed each data sheet in order to categorize the life as upper class, middle class, or lower class. I considered people upper class if they were wearing rich garments, had people waiting on them, or were directing the activities of others—or if they made any mention of the fact that they held a high position in the society they lived in. I classified them as middle class if, in a past life, they were engaged in any kind of craft or had a position of authority, however lowly. I reasoned that "middle class" essentially describes those who do not have to gather food but instead are fed, because the service they are performing for their social group gives them the right to have necessities provided by others. If a subject reported that he was carving wood, constructing buildings, or acting as a leader of a small group of soldiers, he was classified as middle class. It was more difficult to classify the female lives, but here I went on the basis of whether or not the architecture or their houses or the household utensils they reported were of better than humble quality. I classified as lower class any subject who was a member of a primitive tribe, was a soldier who had no authority over any other soldiers, or who was clearly a peasant working on the land. I did have lives as slaves reported, especially in the early time periods, and these I classified as lower class.

When I compiled the social class figures for each of the time periods and plotted them on a graph, a clear pattern emerged. (See Figure 1.) The upper class was very small—less than 10 percent in every time period I measured. The largest percentage of upper-class lives (9.4 percent) occurred in the period of the 1700s. I realized that this high figure for the 1700s was probably an error on my part. The subjects I classified as upper class were wearing satin and velvet clothing and their household utensils seemed of fine quality, but I discovered that many a subject dressed in silks and velvet, and eating from fine metal or pottery plates, lived in a fairly humble home. Apparently, it was a matter of honor in seventeenth-century Europe to dress as elaborately as possible, even on a modest income. This finding of "fancy clothes above one's station" in the 1700s was true not only in my first sample of eight hundred subjects, but also in the second sample of three hundred cases.

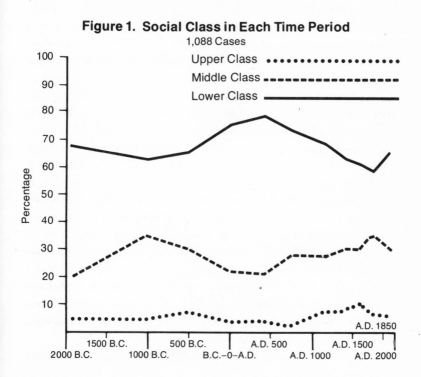

Figure 1. Social Class in Each Time Period
1,088 Cases

The number of middle class lives varied according to the time period. I believe this is because the numbers of artisans or craftsmen in any society is the measure of its level of civilization. Only in some time periods were the societies developed enough to afford not only the rulers (upper class) and the ruled (lower class), but an in-between group that produced the goods of the society and managed its trade. A glance at Figure 1 will show that the middle class reached its peak in 1000 B.C., and did not attain the same level again until the 1700s.

Most of the lives as craftsmen and traders in 1000 B.C. were centered around the eastern Mediterranean region—in Greece, Crete, Mesopotamia, and what is now Turkey. These people made art objects of all kinds and worked with precious metals. According to my data, there was much trading at that time; my subjects reported crowded harbors and marketplaces. Occasionally, a subject would be a trader working the trade routes in that region.

The saying "The poor we always have with us" is certainly borne out by my data. The lower class constituted between 60 and 77 percent of all lives in all the time periods covered. (See Table 1.) If my subjects were fantasizing, their fantasies were bleak and barren. The great majority of my subjects went through their lives wearing rough homespun garments, living in crude huts, eating bland cereal grain with their fingers from wooden bowls. Some of these lives were spent as primitive food-gatherers or nomadic hunters. But the majority of lower class lives in all time periods belonged to people who farmed the land in whatever part of the world they found themselves. Producing food for themselves and the others around them was the major occupation of a large majority of my subjects. If they were fantasizing these past lives, why would they choose such drudgery to recall?

None of my subjects reported a past life as a historical personage. It is possible that if they had recalled such a life, they might have been embarrassed to report it. I had several high priests and one person who reported seeing himself as a Pharaoh of Egypt, but their percentage in the sample was very low. The 7 percent who

Table 1. Social Class in Each Time Period
Based on 1,088 Reported Past Lives

Time Period	Group	Social Classes (in Percentages)		
		Upper	Middle	Lower
2000 B.C.	1 and 2	5	28	67
Total		5	28	67
1000 B.C.	1	4	33	63
1000 B.C.	2	9	36	65
Total		5	34	61
500 B.C.	1	8	30	62
500 B.C.	2	0	28	72
Total		6	30	64
A.D. 25	1	3	20	77
A.D. 25	2	5	27	68
Total		3	22	75
A.D. 400	1	4	20	76
A.D. 400	2	0	18	82
Total		3	20	77
A.D. 800	1	2	25	73
A.D. 800	2	0	37	63
Total		2	27	71
A.D. 1200	1	6	24	70
A.D. 1200	2	6	30	64
Total		6	26	68
A.D. 1500	1	7	28	65
A.D. 1500	2	12	36	52
Total		8	30	62
A.D. 1700	1	8	29	63
A.D. 1700	2	12	33	55
Total		10	30	60
A.D. 1850	1	6	32	62
A.D. 1850	2	6	38	56
Total		7	34	59
1900s	1	7	30	63
1900s	2	5	30	65
Total		6	30	64

reported upper class lives did not feel them to be particularly pleasant. Often the data sheet for such a life had a comment like, "That was a difficult life because I had so many responsibilities. I was glad to leave that body." Some of the happiest lives reported were those of peasants or primitives.

Race in Past Lives

I classified each of my data sheets for each time period by race. I was curious to know if my subjects, who were nearly all white middle class Californians, would see themselves as members of the white race in past lives. If past-life recall was fantasy, I would probably find a higher percentage of the white race in past time periods than history would suggest was true. I also wanted to check on the theory that past-life recall is genetic memory. Is it possible that somehow our DNA molecules, the carriers of our heredity, can contain all the past memories of our racial strain? If the genetic-memory hypothesis were true, my subjects should have been primarily Caucasian.

As can be seen in Figure 2, most of my subjects were not Caucasian in their past lives. It was often difficult to determine their exact racial strain. As I puzzled through the data sheets, trying to classify my subjects according to race in the early B.C. time periods, I became aware of how complicated racial designations are. I classified my subjects as to race on the basis of where they reported living, the color of their skin, and the color and texture of their hair. I found that I had to combine African and Near Eastern races because they intermingled in early time periods. The tight, curly hair characteristic now of the black race seemed to characterize many of the Egyptians. A darker skin tone than I had expected also characterized many of the Near Easterners. For convenience, then, I lumped together the African and Near Eastern into one overall racial type. Skin color ranged from black to a dark olive skin tone and the hair type from tightly curled to wavy, but not straight.

Figure 2. Race in Past Lives
1,088 Cases

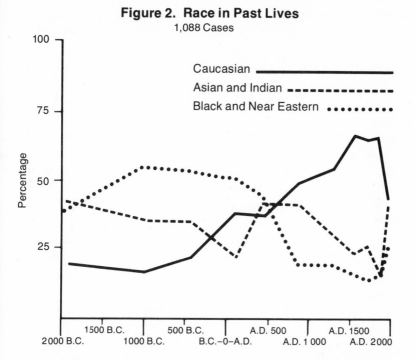

The next race category that I decided upon was Asian and Indian. I found that many of my subjects in Asia reported having coarse, very straight dark hair and a yellowish cast to the skin. Many of my subjects in the Far East described the skin color as reddish-yellow. Since the few subjects I had as American Indians described the same skin color and hair, I decided that, for my purposes, these races should be combined. The Caucasian race is characterized primarily by a much lighter skin color, from light olive to white. The hair type ranged from wavy to straight, but the color was usually light brown. I found that this racial type existed across the northern reaches of Central Asia, as well as being clearly evident around the northern Mediterranean region and Europe.

Figure 2 illustrates the interesting patterns of the races in different time periods in the past. In 2000 B.C. only about 20 percent of the sample were Caucasians. Most of these lives were in the northern Mediterranean region around Greece and Crete, with a scattering of Caucasians through Central Asia in the mountains and northern portion of that area. About 40 percent of my subjects in 2000 B.C. were black and Near Eastern. While there were some lives lived as blacks in Africa, most of these were a Near Eastern type that ranged from North Africa across to Mesopotamia. There are nearly as many Asian and Indian racial types in 2000.

By 1000 B.C. 55 percent of my subjects experienced lives among the black and Near Eastern races. Many of these were in the region from Egypt across to Mesopotamia, where the population seemed to be most heavily concentrated in that period. The Asian and Indian lives decrease somewhat in 1000 B.C., as the reports of lives in Persia and Central Asia declined. Again in 1000 B.C., there were slightly fewer Caucasian lives. The 18 percent of my subjects who were Caucasian in that period seemed to be largely in the region around the Aegean Sea in the civilizations of Cyprus, Crete, and the mainland regions around Turkey.

By 500 B.C., the number of Caucasians had increased to 23 percent of the sample. There seemed to be an increase in the civilization around the Greek islands, and this percentage also includes Caucasian lives lived around the Adriatic Sea in what is now Yugoslavia over to Italy. The bulk of the population was still in the Near East and Africa in 500 B.C., but the population of Asia seemed to remain stable. The Asian and Indian, and the Black and Near Eastern, races still far outnumbered the whites in my sample.

By A.D. 25, the three racial types were more evenly represented. Again, there were more lives lived in the Near Eastern regions, where population was densest. There was a decrease in the number of Asian lives in A.D. 25 in my sample. The number of Caucasian lives increased greatly, and now Caucasian is the second highest racial type in the sample. This appears to represent an increase in lives lived around Italy and Greece, together with a slight increase in the number of lives in the Central Asian steppes.

There is a curious change on my graph of races by A.D. 400.

The three races seem to be nearly completely balanced with one third of the sample Caucasian, one third Asian, and one third black and Near Eastern. For the time span A.D. 400 to 1850, the graph shows a rise in the number of Caucasian lives reported by my subjects. There is a steady increase in the population in Europe, with more and more lives in northern Europe reported. There is a corresponding decrease in the percentage of lives lived in Africa and the Near East, and the same phenomenon is evident with the Asian lives. There is a peak of Indian lives lived around A.D. 800, but these were reported in Central and South America. According to my data, this may mark the height of an early civilization in South America.

An odd change in racial types occurs in the 1900s, according to the data. In 1850, 69 percent of my subjects were white. In the sample of lives reported from 1900 to 1945, nearly a third are reported as Asian. Of all the findings in my study, this has caused me the greatest perplexity.

I had only forty-five subjects who reported a past life in the twentieth century. Since the average age of my subjects was about thirty—so that most of them were born after 1945—it would seem that the people who reported past lives in this century must have been reborn quickly into their current lifetimes. I went over the data sheets for the lifetimes lived in the 1900s to see if I could find a reason for such a racial switch. Genetic memory can certainly be ruled out. Many blond subjects in 1975 to 1977 were black or Asian in their most immediate past lives.

I found that the subjects experiencing a past life in the twentieth century had an unusually high rate of violent deaths. In looking through the data sheets, it became obvious that the reason for this was the number of subjects who were killed in World Wars I and II, or in civil wars in Asia in the twentieth century. Could it be that those killed violently in war incarnate very quickly after their death? The knotty problem of how much "time" there is between incarnations was difficult to research. I had explored this area with my individual subjects, and found that the time between lifetimes ranged from four months to two hundred years, with the average subject returning to reexperience life after an interval of fifty-two years. If this finding from my individual regressions was true, it would mean that only a small percentage of my subjects in the here-and-now in 1974 through 1977 could have had time to be reborn. Such a conclusion seemed to be borne out by my group data, which showed that only 45 subjects experienced a past life in the twentieth century whereas 318 had been alive in the 1800s.

But why the sudden change in race in our own time period? I noted that it had been about two thousand years since the last "switch" in races had taken place. I noticed that black and Near Eastern lives were on an upswing in the 1900s, so it wasn't only Asian lives that increased in the twentieth century. I still have no real explanation for the phenomenon. But I like to think that the Global Village that Marshall McLuhan describes is more than just a cultural phenomenon. Perhaps we are reaching a new kind of world consensus, because we are all breaking out of the cultural limitations of our experiences in past lives. Could it be that there are a lot of Iowa Methodists being reborn in Communist China?

The material on social class and race was interesting. But I found it difficult to research the question of the racial distribution of populations in such time periods as 1000 B.C. All we had to go on were guesses about the population then, because no one was taking censuses in those times. When I checked the data sheets for inaccuracies, I was reminded again of how difficult it is to pinpoint facts from the distant past. We know much less of our history as human beings than we care to admit. The history that was available to me for checking was dominated by Western cultural presumptions about past time periods. Even the field of archeology—which I had looked to to provide solid, scientific evidence of the past—proved to be inadequate. There have been so many new discoveries in archeology within the past ten years that the reference books I used were often outdated by new discoveries.

An example of the difficulties involved in checking can be seen by referring to the case of one subject who was in China in 1000 B.C. She had no money when she was at the marketplace; when she looked down at her hand, she saw tiny wooden objects. "They seemed carved," she recalled. "One was like a little bowl, and one looked like a small loaf of bread or something." I had been unable to find any references to tiny carved objects used as money, so I was tempted to put this response in the category of Inaccuracies. But I realized I could not disprove that this was a form of money used in ancient times, so I kept the data sheet in my collection. It wasn't until many months later that I came across an article in *Scientific American* reporting finds in the Mesopotamia-Persia region. Archeologists had discovered small clay objects apparently used as money in the time period around 1000 B.C. True, my subject was in China, and her objects were wooden rather than clay. But wooden objects would disintegrate long before an archeologist could discover them, while clay objects could well have survived. The exchange of small symbolic objects formed a bridge between barter and a coin system in Mesopotamia. Apparently, this sequence had also occurred in China. Once again, what seemed to be a mistake was shown to be possibly true.

Where could I find information that was not subject to the inaccuracies or unknowns of history and archeology?

Sex Distribution in Each Time Period

I reasoned that I needed at least one biological fact about the past against which to check my evidence. I knew that in any given time period in the past, roughly half of the population was male and half female. This is a biological fact, true of all mammals, including man. I decided to check each time period and determine how many regressions were to male lives and how many to female lives. If past-life recall was fantasy, I would expect to have more male lives: Surveys show that the average citizen, given the opportunity, would prefer to live life as a male. Against this likelihood that fantasy would produce more male lives, I had the situation in which 78 percent of my subjects in the first group were women. Would women be more likely to see themselves as women in a past life?

Thus, there were many imponderables surrounding this question of what sex one would choose in living a past life. Nevertheless, my data, as shown in Figure 3, are quite conclusive. Regardless of the sex they had had in the current lifetime, when regressed to the past, my subjects split neatly and evenly into 50.3 percent male and 49.7 percent female lives. When this finding emerged in my first sample group, I wanted very much to see if it would prove to be true in another sample group. It could be that 28 percent of my female subjects preferred to think of themselves as male, and that was why I had gotten the 50–50 ratio. So in my second sample group of three hundred cases, I had a much closer ratio

Figure 3. Sex Distribution in Each Time Period
804 Cases, Sample Group One

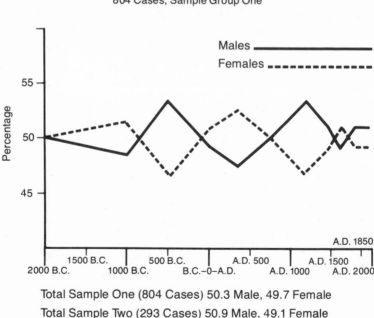

Total Sample One (804 Cases) 50.3 Male, 49.7 Female
Total Sample Two (293 Cases) 50.9 Male, 49.1 Female

of males to females in their here-and-now lives; 45 percent of my subjects were male in the second sample, and 55 percent female. But when I regressed them, I once again found the virtual 50–50 split—this time, 50.9 percent male and 49.1 percent female. This result, I feel, is the strongest objective evidence I have yet discovered that when people are hypnotized and taken to past lives, they are tapping some real knowledge of the past.

Clothing Worn in Past Lives

One of the things that surprised me about my data was the primitive nature of most of the clothing my subjects reported wearing. Underclothing of any kind was rare; often they wore nothing but a loosely woven tunic or robe. Primitive peoples tended to wear animal skins if they lived in northern climates, and often wore nothing at all if they lived in warm climates. Most garments did not seem to be sewn or "manufactured" in any way. The clothing most frequently described was a length of woven cloth with a hole in the middle for the head.

Because it was difficult to graph various types of clothing described by my subjects, I examined the data carefully and decided upon a scheme for demonstrating the nature of the clothing worn in the four-thousand-year period covered by my research. I made one category that of sewn garments. For women, these were dresses or pantaloons (I found there were a number of women, in the Middle East and also in India, who wore a kind of loose, gauzy pants.) Any subject who wore dresses or pants and shirts was considered to be wearing outfits closer to those we wear in our own time period. A second category I devised was draped garments. It seems that draped cloth—sometimes of a very fine weave, sometimes rough—was a very common form of dress in the past. Occasionally, these garments would be colored and patterned, but only rarely, and only in the area around India. In the Mediterranean area, and also in Egypt, the draped garments seemed to be light in color, with no decoration.

The third category included all subjects who were wearing rough animal hides or simple, loosely woven tunics. These tunics were of the serape type with a hole in the middle for the head.

Figure 4 illustrates the incidence of these types of clothing down through the centuries. In 2000 B.C., very few subjects were wearing pants. Between 1500 B.C. and 1000 B.C. the wearing of pants first increased and then diminished. All the subjects reporting wearing of pants in that period were in the area of·what is now Iran and on up through the Caucasus Mountains. The type of pants outfit detailed in my reports was worn by the Parthians and the Scythians, as I learned when I looked up clothing of this description in a book of the history of costumes. As the civilization of the Scythians and Parthians diminished, the occurrence of draped garments increased. I considered Egyptian garments to be draped, but they seemed to be of two primary kinds. One was essentially like a

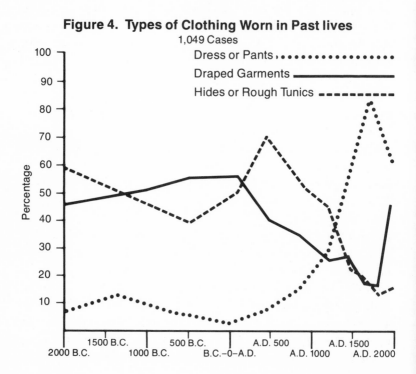

Figure 4. Types of Clothing Worn in Past lives

tunic, worn to the knees or to the ankles, and generally made of finely woven cloth in an off-white color. My middle class and upper class subjects in Egypt wore this kind of garment. The poorer classes in Egypt, especially beginning around 1000 B.C., were clad in a strange kind of diaper arrangement covering the body from the waist to the mid-thigh. Upon examining Egyptian drawings, I saw illustrations of both these costumes. It is of interest to note here that the workers are generally shown wearing the draped, diaperlike garment, while the overseers are in knee-length garments. When royalty is shown in everyday activities in pictures of Egyptian life that have come down to us, the garment they wear is down to the ankles. My findings are entirely consistent with the pictorial evidence of Egyptian clothing.

It is of course possible that many of my subjects could have seen the same illustrations in museums or in books that I did in my research, but it is surprising to me that they made no errors. If they were poor, they wore the diaperlike arrangement; if not poor, they reported the other type of clothing. Would all these subjects have known the specific facts about clothing in ancient Egypt? I don't think it's likely.

The wearing of draped garments reached its height around the time of Imperial Rome. I received many descriptions of the Roman toga, and the garments worn in Greece in the same period were similar. By A.D. 400 the draped toga had apparently gone out of style. There was a slight increase in the number of subjects wearing pants, apparently reflecting those whose lives were lived in the Islamic civilization on the southern shores of the Mediterranean Sea, from A.D. 400 to 1200. The garments they described are similar to those we have all seen in illustrations of the *Arabian Nights.*

By A.D. 1200 pants of the type we know today began to appear in my data. They were often described as short pants or knickers, and long legging-type stockings were worn with them, especially in the European regressions from A.D. 1200 through the 1700s. The long pants that we know today in our culture did not show up consistently in my sample until the 1850s.

The use of hides or rough tunics as apparel appears to indicate a low level of civilization. More sophisticated cultures around the Mediterranean Sea through Central Asia to India and China wore the draped garments, whereas primitive people apparently utilized hides for garments. Most of the hides were unscraped and were not described as "leather" until around A.D. 25. The period of the Middle Ages—from A.D. 400 to A.D. 1200—showed first an increase in these primitive clothing materials and then a decrease as the Renaissance began.

An examination of Figure 4 shows a strange reversal of the general trend of the data in the twentieth century. By 1850, 73 percent of my subjects were wearing dresses or pants, the number of draped garments had decreased to around 15 percent of the sample, and rough hides and tunics constituted only 12 percent. The reversal of the clothing type in the twentieth century is due to a peculiarity I discovered in my data: More than one third of my subjects had lived in Asia in their twentieth-century lives, and Africa and the Near East accounted for 25 percent of my subjects in the same time period. That meant that they were wearing draped garments in the lives they lived in Asia and the Near East prior to 1940— which does confirm what we know about clothing styles. Western dress did not extend throughout the world until the period just before World War II, and even today there are parts of the world where draped garments are preferred.

Types of Footwear in Each Time Period

A glance at Figure 5 shows clearly that the great majority of my subjects either walked barefoot or wore crude sandals, hides, and rags around their feet until A.D. 1700. It wasn't until 1850 that a clear majority were wearing boots, shoes, or slippers. No wonder children kick off their shoes all the time!

Even upper and middle class subjects of high civilizations in past time periods did not wear complete foot coverings; they wore delicately wrought sandals instead. The exception to this general rule is the Far East: In China, I find cloth slippers going back as far as 2000 B.C. The use of cloth shoes did not appear in Europe

Figure 5. Types of Footwear in Each Time Period

802 Cases

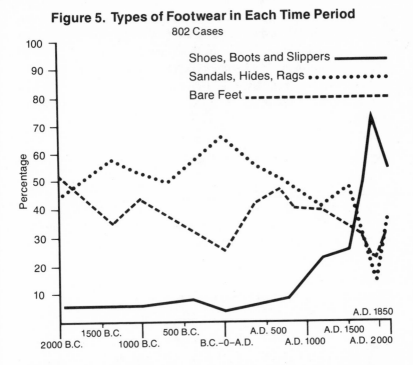

in my data until 1400. Then, cloth shoes and slippers were as common as boots until the 1500s. Apparently, Marco Polo's explorations brought the Chinese shoe style to Europe, and it spread through Europe from 1300 to 1500. This is the kind of suggestive data that emerges again and again from my research. Could all of my subjects have thought about this sequence of events, and decided that if they were in medieval Europe they would be wearing cloth slippers? It is difficult for me to believe that 1,100 past-life regressions could be so consistent and accurate. If people are weaving into past-life recall under hypnosis things they have seen or read, they are certainly doing a magnificent job. It is worth noting that many of my subjects express some dismay at the difficulty they have in pinpointing their historical periods. Yet how accurately they report the small details of the past!

As my data show, we have another strange reversal of trends

in the twentieth century, again accounted for by the switch in races evident in the data from the early twentieth century. My subjects in Asia were less likely to wear shoes and boots and more likely to be barefoot or wearing some type of sandal. Thus, this curious finding of a switch in races and cultures in our own time period is supported by all of my graphs and is consistent through all the variables I have tested.

Types of Food Eaten in Each Time Period

Figure 6 illustrates clearly that until 1850, over half of all my subjects in all time periods were eating cereal grains as their primary food. I chose to combine cereal and vegetables to illustrate the products of agriculture. The great majority of my subjects in all

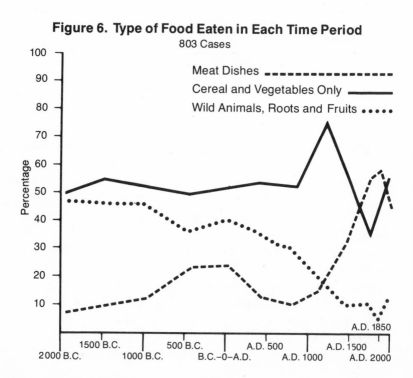

Figure 6. Type of Food Eaten in Each Time Period

time periods earned their living from the land. Primitive peoples reported eating wild animals, roots, and fruits, such as berries that they had gathered, but organized agriculture resulting in the production of cereal grains is evident in the data from 2000 B.C. to the present.

The designation "meat dishes" indicates those past lives in which subjects reported eating domestic fowl or other domestic animals. I took this as a measure of civilization; animal husbandry is as important as farming in this regard.

As can be seen from the data, a high point of civilization, as indicated by the types of food eaten, came between 500 B.C. and A.D. 1. The meat eaten then was generally either a domesticated fowl of some kind or lamb. Not one subject reported eating beef until the late 1500s. The data on types of food eaten clearly shows a reduction in the lavishness of the food supply during what we call the Dark Ages, from A.D. 25 through to about 1200. But organized agriculture apparently increased during this time, because the line for cereal grains rises steadily and the line for the gathering of wild animals, roots, and fruits decreases. Essentially, this means that there were fewer primitives in my sample from 1000 B.C. down to the present.

It wasn't until 1700 that as many people were eating meat dishes as were eating cereal grains, and not until 1850 did the diet of my subjects include meat more frequently than it did cereals alone.

Again the reversal in the twentieth century occurs. Subjects who were in Asia and the Near East in the twentieth century ate less meat and more cereal grains or fruits.

The type of cereal grain eaten was often unique to the part of the world in which my subjects found themselves. Most frequently it was eaten as a mush—ground up and then mixed with water and warmed. Eaten along with the cereal grains was a primitive type of bread that was apparently unleavened and that some of my subjects thought was much like the "pita" bread that we know today from the Near East.

As a general rule, my subjects were eating such bland and uninteresting meals that I wasn't surprised when, one day in a workshop, a young man commented, "I'll never say bad things about Mc-Donald's again. Food now is certainly a lot better than it used to be!"

I asked my subjects whether the food they ate was spicy or bland, because I hoped to get information on the use of spices in past time periods. My data showed that few subjects tasted any spice at all in their foods, especially salt. Spices were found only in the meals of the wealthy, particularly in the Mediterranean regions and the Western Hemisphere. In India, sometimes even the poor had condiments in their food.

In my sample, the best meals of all were found in China. From very early times, my subjects reported that Chinese cooking was delicious; although here, too, few spices were used, there was a greater variety in the meals reported.

I asked my subjects to taste the food. Some were able to report taste sensations much more vividly than others. In part, this might have been because so many of them were eating bland cereals in their past lives, but it may also mean that under hypnosis the sense of taste is less vivid than such senses as vision and touch. It was interesting to me that about 8 percent of my subjects reported that the food they ate tasted spoiled in some way. This was especially true about the meats they ate.

"Ugh! The meat that I'm eating tastes spoiled," was the kind of remark I got. "I think it's lamb or something like that. Very unpleasant." Subjects who were eating wild animals reported the spoiled taste less often, but might comment, "It's some kind of small animal, like a rodent of some kind. It's very greasy, and as I bite into it I can feel the grease on my mouth." Few of the primitive tribes ate any large animals: they seemed to rely on small creatures such as squirrels for their meals.

Many of my subjects in the B.C. periods were eating fruits, especially in the region around Mesopotamia. Interestingly, they experienced the flavor of the fruits as something new to their taste buds. "It's some kind of fruit, rather like a melon," a subject would report. "But it tastes different. I never tasted anything like that." Two fruits that we know today were reported in past time periods: the fig, which apparently tasted then much as it does now, and the grape. Vegetables that we have no knowledge of today were also reported. Some of the primitive tribesmen ate roots that occurred naturally in the areas where they gathered food. In my sample, the turnip showed up in Europe to a surprising extent.

Once, when I was talking to a subject about her regression, which had taken place six months previously, she reported that in the past life she had been eating a raw turnip. "I've never tasted a turnip," she said, "and I don't quite know how I knew it was a turnip. But it just looked like one." She described how several months later she had been eating in a restaurant with her husband when his meal came to the table: "There was some strange white vegetable, with a sauce on it, on his plate. I like to sample his food as well as mine, so I tasted it. I told him that it tasted just like the turnips I had eaten in my past-life regression. We called the waitress over, and she confirmed that the vegetable on the plate was indeed turnips."

I asked my subjects what utensils they were using in a past life at the evening meal, and the great majority said they ate with their fingers. Typically, a subject reported, "I'm using the first three fingers of my right hand and scooping up the food. There doesn't seem to be any utensil."

From among those subjects who found themselves using a utensil, some very interesting data emerged. Covering the time period 500 B.C. through A.D. 400, I had over thirty-five reports of a kind of shallow wooden spoon that resembled a scoop or a shovel. This eating implement, which seems to have been a primitive forerunner of our modern-day spoon, was used around the Mediterranean Sea, but also appeared in Europe in A.D. 400. I had an additional five cases of a much deeper spoon that looked more like a dipper, which was used in the Near East from Egypt across to Lebanon, again in the period around A.D. 25. It too was made of wood. There were some reports of two-pronged forks in the area around Rome and in Egypt in A.D. 25, but their use appeared to be limited to the rich.

As I moved up through the time periods, I discovered a fascinating phenomenon: As more and more of my subjects became middle class and lived in civilized areas, the use of eating utensils increased. By 1500, I had my first report of a three-pronged fork. By the 1700s over half of my subjects were using the three-pronged fork for their evening meals. This utensil, which seems to have been larger than our modern fork and was usually made of metal, continued to show up through the regressions until the time period around 1800. It was in 1790 that my first example of a four-pronged fork appeared, and by 1850 the majority of my subjects were eating with such a fork. A few subjects still had three-pronged forks, which were often described as being made of silver and were apparently "antiques" from the previous century. In all, 214 subjects reported the use of forks as eating utensils.

Though the four-pronged fork was prominent in the nineteenth-century regressions, the most common eating implement throughout all the time periods was a simple wooden spoon. According to my sample, the use of wood for household utensils was very extensive, a fact that intrigued me because I had not run across it in my study of archeology. Of course, archeologists would not be likely to discover wooden articles because they would have disintegrated before the researchers arrived to dig out the remains of an old civilization. As a matter of fact, my subjects reported that wood was very seldom used in building houses, except as supporting beams. The scarcity of wood as a building material probably related to the fact that so many subjects were in civilizations around the Near East and Asia, where trees were rare. Apparently, the wood that did exist was used primarily for household implements and furniture.

Types of Plates Used in Each Time Period

Figure 7 illustrates the types of plates used in each time period. As is evident, the great majority of my subjects used wooden plates, leaves, or gourds, or ate out of a communal pot. It was not until 1700 that more subjects were using china plates than were using the more primitive types of container. By 1850, 59 percent were using china and pottery plates, but even in this advanced time period, there was extensive use of wood.

Interestingly, Figure 7 shows that metal plates were more common than pottery in my sample until 1700. The metal was variously described as "shiny, dark gray," "looks like pewter," "some kind of metal, I can't tell what kind." Pottery plates, of the sort museums exhibit in their ancient civilization collections, were restricted in my sample to the very rich. In such places as India, even the wealthy still ate from a communal platter or pot rather than from individual serving bowls or plates. Apparently, the pottery used in ancient civilizations was reserved for storage or for serving; the dinner plate considered essential in our modern time periods was quite

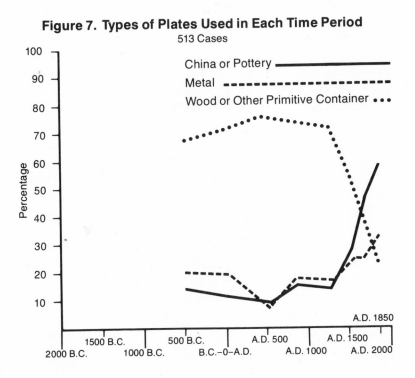

Figure 7. Types of Plates Used in Each Time Period
513 Cases

unknown in the past. This is especially interesting because my deliberate suggestion under hypnosis was, "Look down at what you're
eating from. Is it a plate? a bowl?" The fact that so many of my
subjects saw no such thing, even when I directed their attention
to it, tells us something about suggestion under hypnosis. They
saw what they saw regardless of my instructions. They were eating
from leaves, they were dipping their hands in communal bowls,
or they were simply eating with their hands. If past-life recall is
fantasy, one would expect that all of them would have seen the
plates or bowls I suggested. This is a small item of evidence, but
it is of the kind that I find most interesting.

Whenever my subjects try to follow my suggestions under hypnosis but are unable to do so, what they report has the ring of truth
to it.

Population in Past Time Periods

One of the most common objections to the theory of reincarnation
is that the population of the world doubled from A.D. 25 to 1500,
doubled again by 1800, and by now has quadrupled. If there were
reincarnation, critics contend, then the population of the earth
would have been much larger in the past than we know to be the
case. Therefore, people who propose the theory of reincarnation
have to account for these population differences in past time periods.

I find this a cogent argument against the possibility of reincarnation if we are thinking in terms of unique personalities who are
living series of lives. It was difficult to devise an experimental
method for checking the population of the earth in past time periods.
One reason I chose my technique of going back four thousand
years and choosing ten different time periods was to see if I could
get any data on this vexing question. I reasoned that although
people might have images from certain time periods in the past,
they would be able to experience past life in only one time period
each trip. By graphing the time periods they chose, I could get
some indication of the population of the earth from 2000 B.C. to
the present.

Figure 8 is the graph of my subjects who were alive in each of the time periods in the past. I say "were alive" because they reported experiencing lives in those time periods. It is theoretically possible, of course, that they could have chosen any other time period and also experienced lives then. Essentially, each subject was told to experience three past lives, and was allowed to choose more or less at random the time periods in which to experience being alive in a body.

As can be seen from Figure 8, the population of the world does indeed double from A.D. 400 to 1600 and then doubles again by 1850. What an extraordinary finding! These findings from the first

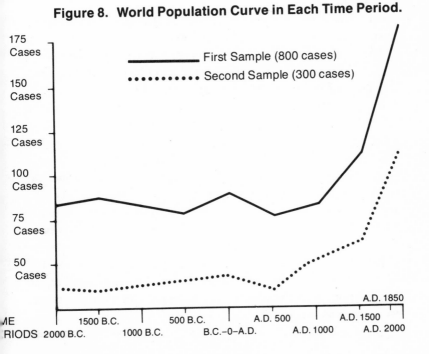

Figure 8. World Population Curve in Each Time Period.

eight hundred cases were reproduced in my second sample of three hundred cases.

Were my subjects, as a group, actually representing the world's population at any given time? It seems unlikely, yet the consistency of the population curves resulting from my data do suggest that I may well have been tapping a representative sample from the past.

As can be seen from Figure 8, the population of the world remained fairly steady until A.D. 25. There was a slight increase at that time, which might have been due to the Roman Empire's ability to provide bread and circuses to an otherwise starving population. When Rome fell, the population of the world declined, and stayed lower than it had been in the B.C. periods, until about A.D. 1200. It was in 1200 that the population of the world, according to my sample, began to rise rapidly, and the rate of the rise remained slow but steady until 1500. In 1500 the population began to rise very steeply indeed, until by 1600 the world population was double what it had been in earlier time periods. The population increase curve rose even more steeply after 1600.

Was it a coincidence that my data repeated this estimate of the world's population patterns through history? I reasoned that it was possible that my subjects were experiencing more lives in recent time periods because they had more data available to them with which to construct fantasies. Thus more of them might choose 1850 to construct a past-life fantasy than would choose 500 B.C. This is a possibility that cannot be ruled out. Another possible reason for this curve is that the more recent the time period, the more past lives might be remembered vividly. However, my data refute such a finding. People alive in 500 B.C. experience things just as vividly as those alive in 1850. The emotional quality of the regressions does not differ.

If I could extend my curve from 1850 to 1977, it would run clear off the page. This would mean that the population quadrupled again by modern times, which is indeed the case, according to world demographers.

Does the fact that my findings on subjects alive in past time periods reproduce the estimated population curve of the earth constitute proof of reincarnation? I would say that the data are very suggestive, though in no way conclusive. But at least I now have an answer to those who question reincarnation because of low population densities in past time periods. It is now possible to say that the evidence of 1,100 past-life regressions does indeed show far fewer people alive in the past than today.

The Death Experience in Each Time Period

People who have experienced "clinical death" and then been revived have reported out-of-body experiences during that time. Dr. Raymond Moody and other researchers have collected data on the "death experience" in hundreds of such cases. The studies show that among the subjects who experience clinical death, 10 to 25 percent of them later recall that they found themselves out of their body and had a deep feeling of peace and freedom from pain. During the experience, they look down and see others around their body. After a brief time of hovering over their bodies, they report moving through a tunnel toward the light. They seem to be soaring up toward that light, and when they reach it they are greeted by loved ones and often by some sort of a religious figure. This might be an angel, or a dead relative, or it might be Jesus. Some of the subjects who are clinically dead and later revived report they are told they must return to their body.

I asked all of my subjects to experience death in a past life, in order to determine whether their reports corresponded with those found by other researchers. While it is certainly possible that at least some of my subjects were aware of stories about the death experience, it is unlikely that all of them had read Dr. Moody's book, *Life After Life,* or read stories about the death experience. I can't rule out the possibility that under hypnosis my subjects are reporting what they have read, but again the universality of their experience suggests that past knowledge could not have produced such unanimity.

I asked my subjects to write on their data sheets what they

experienced at death—specifically the nature of the death and the emotion experienced following the death. I did not suggest that they would see a light, that they would see anyone they knew before death, or that they would be in a tunnel.

Table 2 illustrates the positive nature of the death experience for almost all subjects under hypnosis who went to their death in a past life. An average of 49 percent experienced feelings of deep calm and peace and accepted their death with no difficulty. Another 30 percent experienced very positive feelings of joy and release. An average of 20 percent experienced seeing their bodies after their death, and floating above the body while watching the activity around it. There is no doubt from the report of my subjects after they awoke from the hypnosis that death was the best part of the trip. Again and again they reported how pleasant it was to die, and what a sense of release they had after they left their bodies. Even subjects who had had considerable fear of death prior to the workshop told me that after having experienced death in a past life, they lost the fear of death in their current life.

"Dying was like being released, like going home again. It was as though a great burden had been lifted when I left my body and floated up toward the light. I felt affection for the body I had lived in in that lifetime, but it was so good to be free!" This was a very common response to the death experience in my sample.

The emotions that my subjects experienced at death were so strong that they were reflected in their here-and-now bodies. "Tears of joy came to me when you took us to the death experience," one subject said. "I could feel the tears trickling down my cheeks in the here-and-now, but my whole body felt so light right after I died."

About 10 percent of my subjects reported feeling upset or emotions of sorrow at death. They were experiencing such emotions because of the manner of their death or the people they were leaving behind them. They found themselves very surprised to be outside their bodies and attempted to maintain contact with their loved ones from their out-of-body state. "I feel so bad because I'm leaving

Table 2. The Death Experience in Each Time Period
Based on 1,088 Reported Past Lives
(Expressed in Percentages)

Time Period	Type of Death				Emotion at Death Experience			
	Natural	Natural or Accidental	Violent	None Experienced	Calm, Accepting	Joy, Release	Sees Body	Fear, Sorrow
2000 B.C.	73	16	11	0	41	37	17	5
1000	59	12	25	4	44	20	24	12
500	56	18	19	7	46	34	15	5
A.D. 25	64	6	20	10	41	34	17	8
400	55	15	20	10	50	20	22	8
800	64	12	24	0	38	32	26	4
1200	55	16	24	5	39	26	22	13
1500	62	15	19	4	49	28	16	7
1700	64	17	16	3	49	30	6	15
1850	64	13	13	10	58	25	9	8
1900s	47	13	31	9	42	8	33	17

my two children behind," a subject who died in childbirth reported. "I worry about who will take care of them, and I stay around my body trying to comfort my husband."

Another kind of disturbing experience at death was that of being killed accidentally or violently, usually at a young age. "I was hit by a car while I was running across the street," one subject said. "I seemed to continue running across the street, and wasn't really aware that I was dead. Then I felt very frustrated and lost, because I didn't understand what was happening to me. Finally, I was in a place of darkness and then I saw a bright light. Then I went soaring up through the darkness toward the light."

Some of my subjects who expressed negative feelings at death were fighting in a war: "I was fighting and then my body crumpled. I kept on fighting, but I couldn't seem to affect anything going on around me. I was still on the battlefield, but then I seemed to be joined by others who had died. I couldn't seem to leave that scene."

Some subjects experienced sorrow because of others' grief at their death. The sorrow was not for themselves but for the people who remained on earth.

About 25 percent reported a brief period of darkness followed by light. More subjects, about two thirds, experienced soaring up high above their body into a light-filled world, where they were greeted by others and had an instant sense of companionship. One subject reported, "I soared up high in the sky after I left my body. I didn't want to look back. I seemed, then, to be surrounded by others, who were congratulating me in that lifetime. I felt a sense of homecoming and great joy. There was life all around me."

I also checked on the cause of death in each time period because the past-life regressions reported in the literature to date indicate far too many deaths by violence. Many of the past-life regressions I have read about in past-life therapy cases describe violent and unpleasant deaths. I knew that statistically this could not be true, so I wondered whether my sample would produce the same results. If past-life recall is fantasy, then violent death would occur much more frequently than it should, according to statistics on death in the here-and-now world.

As can be seen from Table 2, the overall percentage of natural deaths in all the time periods is 62 percent. While it is difficult to find statistics on causes of death that can be connected with the regions of the world in the time periods I was studying, this seems to be quite a reasonable figure. Because many of my subjects were thirty years or under when they died in past life periods, one would expect more accidental and violent deaths then than today. Still, well over half of all the subjects died from disease or old age.

The percentage of natural or accidental deaths is only an estimate. Many of my subjects said something like, "I'm falling down, and now I seem to be dead." Was this the result of a heart attack or an accident? Unless they were aware of some natural cause for their death, such as a heart attack or difficulty in breathing, I assigned these deaths to the accidental deaths column. The violent deaths, which were 18 percent of the entire sample, were caused by murder, suicide, or attack by an animal.

Table 2 shows that the figures for types of death varied according to time periods. The largest number of violent deaths occurred in two time periods—1000 B.C. and the 1900s. Apparently, there were many minor wars in 1000 B.C., because many of my subjects found themselves dying in skirmishes of one kind or another. The common form of warfare then was not a battle between fixed armies. My subjects reported that they would be living peacefully in a village, when they were suddenly attacked by a small band of marauders. In the twentieth century, the high percentage of violent deaths came from death by bombing. Interestingly, many of my subjects who died in World War II reported dying of smoke inhalation following a bombing attack. Fire seems to have claimed more lives in World War II bombing raids through asphyxiation than through the actual explosions. This corresponds with known facts regarding the bombing raids in World War II, and is one of those small details it is unlikely my subjects would fantasize about.

In looking for data to chart the incidence of natural death as opposed to accidental or violent death, I ran across some interesting figures. The New York City Health Department issued figures on causes of death for nonwhites between the ages of fifteen and twenty-four during 1976. I feel that the results of this survey approximate the experiences of my sample in many of the past-time periods, because people died at a younger age in those times and because the life lived was often as full of danger as is life in New York City today. But, according to these recent figures, you're in more danger living in New York City today than you were living in the jungle in 2000 B.C. In 1976, over half of the deaths of male nonwhite citizens between the ages of fifteen and twenty-four were the result of murder. Fifty-five percent! The figure was 50 percent for female nonwhites. Accidents accounted for another 33 percent of the deaths, and only 22 percent died of natural causes. When I used these figures of New York City deaths in 1976 as a reference point, it seemed clear that my data represented a normal pattern. The number of violent deaths reported for each time period is not out of line with known historical reality.

I believe it is no accident that violent or difficult deaths are uncovered in past-life therapy cases. Probably, past-life deaths that were fraught with negative emotions just prior to the death experience could result in phobias in the current lifetime. I have found this to be true both in individual and group regressions. Many subjects have come to me after the past-life workshops had receded in their memories, and reported that phobias had been dissipated as a result of experience of the death in a past life.

Shirley Kleppe's past-life recall as Marie, described in Chapter 5, enabled her to overcome dizzy spells and an unaccountable urge to run which had troubled her since she was six years old. By reliving the death she experienced as a French girl pursued over the edge of a cliff by angry townspeople, she eradicated the symptoms that had troubled her for so long. Other subjects have reported losing their fear of horses after they experienced a death caused by a horse in a past life, or have lost their fear of water after they relived a death by drowning. It is very difficult to come to any conclusion about the validity of these experiences. To the subject, as noted before, whether or not the past-life recall is valid is of much less importance than the disappearance of a phobic symptom.

Some of my subjects skipped the death experience in the past life, in accordance with my instructions to do so, if they became uncomfortable when I asked them to experience their death. It was interesting to note that the same subject might accept the death experience in two past lives, but block it in a third. It was as though it was the nature of the death that disturbed subjects, not the fact of death itself.

The death experience was apparently at the root of my difficulty in hypnotizing that 10 percent of my subjects who were unable to experience past-life regression. To test the hypothesis that the death experience was blocking their past-life trips, I took ten such subjects into individual hypnosis and worked with them extensively. I found that only two of the ten were able to go under hypnosis individually, so the blocking of the experience was not due to the group condition. After my assurance under hypnosis that they would feel detached and not feel any emotion, these two went to past deaths in their most immediate past lives and described very unpleasant death experiences in those lives. Both had died in World War II, one in an explosion and the other through infection contracted on a South Pacific island. I took both of them to the experience immediately after death, and they expressed the same feelings of lightness and freedom, peace, and even joy that my other subjects had reported. The difficulty was not in being dead; the problem was the highly charged negative emotions they experienced just before their death. Armed with this evidence, I then tried to hypnotize the remaining eight subjects.

Four of the eight were unable to go under hypnosis in any way, so I tried free association. But even with the free association technique, they clearly avoided exploring anything in the subconscious. I therefore concluded that they knew best and that further efforts to obtain information would only upset them. With the remaining four, free association uncovered a fear of death. When I reassured them that we would not explore the death experience, all four went under hypnosis and described past lives.

These findings are suggestive. Past-life recall seems to be available to all of us, if we are motivated to allow it and if our subconscious will permit it. In my sample at least, a block in recalling past lives appears to be related to a fear of reexperiencing the emotions just prior to death in the most immediate past life. That the great majority of my subjects—90 percent—were able to experience death in a past life with no real disturbance, and often with great feelings of joy, suggests that it is only a small minority who suffer continuing problems because of trauma in a past death or deaths. It is probably these subjects whom past-life therapy would help, by breaking through and relieving the pressure caused by these memories.

All the data described in this chapter tended to support the hypothesis that past-life recall accurately reflects the real past rather than that it represents common fantasies. None of the data indicated that fantasy was at work. But of course, this was not enough to prove that past-life recall reflects reality. I needed another kind of evidence.

Would my subjects agree with one another when they were in the same time period and in the same place in the past? Because I hypnotized them in different workshops and at different times, telepathy would not be able to account for similarities in clothing and architecture that they saw in past lives. Would I find any such evidence in the regressions when I analyzed them by time periods and place?

9

LIFE IN THE B.C. PERIODS

Twenty-one percent of my eleven hundred subjects went to lifetimes lived before the birth of Christ. In my first group of eight hundred subjects, 21 percent went to the B.C. time period. In my second sample group of three hundred, 20 percent went to the B.C. time periods. This remarkably close correspondence is mirrored by the percent of my subjects alive in 2000 B.C.: 7 percent in the first sample and 8 percent in the second. In the 1000 B.C. time period and in 500 B.C., the two sample groups were in complete agreement: 7 percent of both sample 1 and sample 2 went to 1000 B.C.; 6 percent of each sample went to 500 B.C. Apparently, civilizations around the time of 2000 B.C. were more heavily populated than those in later time periods.

I looked at my figures for the upper, middle, and lower classes in the three B.C. time periods to see if there was a correspondence between sample group 1 and sample group 2. The figures were remarkably similar in the two samples. In 2000 B.C., 5 percent of the subjects were upper class in both samples. The middle class comprised 26 percent of sample 1 and 30 percent of sample 2, yielding an average of 28 percent middle class in that time period. The lower class percentages averaged out to 67 percent in both samples.

In 1000 B.C., 4 percent of my first sample and 9 percent of my second sample were upper class. The figure for middle class was also quite stable, at 33 percent for sample 1 and 36 percent for sample 2, yielding an average of 34 percent for the entire sample in 1000 B.C. Lower class lives averaged 61 percent. When compared to class distributions in other time periods, this figure means that the B.C. period was somewhat more prosperous than any other period until the 1500s.

The number of artisans, merchants, and other middle class people remained roughly the same—30 percent—in the 500 B.C. period, whereas the upper class increased slightly to 6 percent. Lower class lives totaled 62 percent of the first and 72 percent of the second sample, yielding an average of 65 percent.

It was interesting to me to note where my subjects lived in the 2000 B.C. time period. Only seven of the eighty-four cases in 2000 B.C. found themselves in the Western Hemisphere. Though the location was specified precisely only in one case, internal evidence suggested that another was in the area now the United States (possibly Arizona), and the other six in South America.

One of the lives in Central America sounded very pleasant. My subject found himself a female with long, black, loose hair that had beads tied to it on each side, and was dressed in a leather skirt, but bare from the waist up. The landscape was a valley that looked out on plains, with a river to the left and a forest behind. The buildings "looked like lean-tos made of some kind of twigs." In response to a question about childhood activity, my subject spoke of riding a horse, and added on his data sheet the fact that he felt this was not possible in 2000 B.C. It is interesting to note that the remains of a horse *have* been uncovered in archeological research, which indicates horses were known in the Western Hemisphere as early as 3000 B.C.

The subjects who went to lives in South America in 2000 B.C. (7 percent) described civilizations that sounded much more advanced. One male subject reported the following lifetime: "I'm wearing leather thongs and a long skirt made of some kind of cloth. There seems to be a vest of some sort and an ornate wide belt of metal. My hair is black and down to my mid-neck. My skin is

dark brown. The climate is very warm and comfortable. I see buildings that look like temples. They have smooth stone walls and
steps on each side." The food was a whitish-yellow gruel or corn
mash.

He was learning in childhood to write some type of symbols,
but did not describe them in further detail. He thought that in
his adult life he was involved in making inscriptions or symbols,
a skill to which he devoted his life. He died in his fifties of an
unspecified cause. His religious beliefs in that life taught that "the
spiritual sun is God or a force." The experience of the spirit leaving
the body was "cascading golden light—swirling golden waterfall
of light going over me." The map he saw was Peru.

Another subject also recalled a life in the same region of South
America in 2000 B.C. He too had dark reddish skin and black
hair worn low on the neck, and wore sandals made of leather.
He could not describe his clothing except to say that it was loose.
The buildings he saw were similar to those seen by the first subject,
and he described them as elaborate and beautiful. In childhood
he too learned a form of writing that was expressed by symbols.
In his mature life he was a farmer, but apparently he also made
pots because he recalled putting his symbol on a pot. He also saw
complicated and elaborate designs on the walls of a nearby house.
This subject did not experience his death in much detail, but he
was old when he died and his death appeared to be natural. Like
the subject in Peru, he too had the experience of light at his death.
He wrote in his comments at the bottom of the data sheet: "It
was a very advanced and artistic civilization. It seems out of place
for such a long time ago. I flashed on the date of my death as
2031 B.C. I did see very vividly the Indian man who I was, with
my straight black hair."

Three other subjects who were in South America in 2000 B.C.
all described themselves as being in a jungle climate, being barefooted, and wearing loin cloths. They referred to their skin as dark,
rather than specifying in tones of brown to red. The buildings they
saw were "mud huts" (subject 1); "little round huts, I can see

through the walls between holes" (subject 2); and "straw and mud construction" (subject 3). It is interesting that all saw the same type of construction in the same geographical area in the same time period. All seemed to be eating similar food—a yellowish mushy substance. One of the three described it as a "root, like a potato." Another said that it "looks yellowish, like corn mush." Their activities varied slightly. The two male subjects were sharpening spears and hunting; the woman subject was making an arrowhead and wrapping it.

The experience after death varied, but the two who did experience the death (the third blocked it at my suggestion) described flying high in the air after it occurred. One stated that the religious teaching said he would become a bird spirit. The other two did not report a specific teaching about death, though it is interesting that both described soaring, in contrast to the golden-light experience of the higher civilization in Peru.

The most fascinating of these lives in South America was also lived in the Chile-Peru region in which the civilization was characterized by symbols, at "a time period somewhere before 2000 B.C." It was totally different from all the others in my sample.

The subject was a male, and when he looked down at his feet, he saw "bright smooth metal." "I'm wearing some kind of soft silver-metallic cloth, like a jump suit, from head to toes," he said. "I have no hair and I'm wearing some kind of gloves, and I have long fingers. I am in a mountainous region and the climate is mild." The buildings he saw were "stone and metal, quite tall. They look somehow modern." His childhood activities were composed of operating an electronic board and playing complex computation-block games. For food, he ate "some kind of vegetables and some kind of fruit." He said his mature life was taken up with writing and scholarly activities, and spent in "beautiful surroundings." He reported being old at death and gave the cause as "electrochemical malfunction." He said about his death: "I feel that it is the proper time. I'm not aware of any religious teaching. When my spirit leaves my body, it feels comfortable and soft."

At the bottom of his data sheet, he sketched some fascinating buildings. One was almost pyramid shaped, though more elongated than most pyramids. The other was a cylindrical building with a squared-off walkway going about half way up the building. The chair he drew seemed to have only one wide leg on which the seat rested. His eating tool was a small arrowhead-shaped flat object that looked like a scooper. Was this subject someone from the lost continent of Atlantis, who had traveled to South America and was establishing a civilization there? Was the advanced civilization reported by my two other subjects a decayed version of this original one? Obviously, my data can provide no answers to these questions. But the similar locations do suggest the possibility of a connection.

The group of original reports of hypnotized subjects that follows should give the flavor of past lives in the B.C. periods. As can be seen, questions on the data sheets varied somewhat according to the trip number.

TRIP 2

Sex Female as female
Place Asia
Appearance Black, thick, straight hair. "Dark skin, rather Indianlike. Dark circles under eyes."
Dress Arms bare. Bare feet. "Loosely woven cloth encircling my body."
Landscape and Terrain Very hot and sunny, dry terrain, sparse foliage and sandy soil. Flimsy straw huts, huge leaves for roof, rounded entrance.
Food and Mealtimes "My family and I ate out of enormous bowls either with our hands or with pieces of bread."
Childhood Activities "I was playing in the mud near a narrow body of water. I saw myself working an abacuslike apparatus, trying to learn arithmetic or something to do with numbers."
Mature-Life Activities "Very little energy—very little to do."
Death Died at age 83 in 2083 B.C. "Completely ready—sitting under a tree, my spirit left my body." The religious teaching was that there was an afterlife. After leaving the body, "My soul experienced a state of confusion at first."
Karmic Connections "My brother."

TRIP 2

Sex   Male as female
Place   Babylonia-Mesopotamia
Appearance   Hair is done up in braids on top of head.
Dress   Sandals, long simple dress.
Landscape and Terrain   Adobe buildings, semi-desert-Sumer.
Food and Mealtimes   "Dates, sesame-seed cookies, cucumbers, fruit, grains." Eating utensils were made of clay, which had been baked. The father, a priest, mother and brothers and sister were eating with her.
Childhood Activities   "Weaving on tall loom in large house."
Mature-Life Activities   "Married at 17 to dark, curly-haired man. Lived with parents. Have large land and buildings—canals irrigate fields of barley, wheat, date trees. Became mother of large family, grandchildren." Was well to do, with large flocks and fields.
Death   Died at age 60 of disease. The family gathered to mourn, and "My spirit wanted to comfort them. I stay around, then join husband (dead) and move on in speed of light to new realm of existence." The date of death was 2060 B.C.
Karmic Connections   None mentioned.

TRIP 2

Sex   Female as male
Place   Indian Ocean
Appearance   "Short coarse black hair. Left hand had ring on it."
Dress   Soft animal skins, draped and tied, bare feet.
Landscape and Terrain   "Sand, like desert. Rather cool for desert, pleasantly cool with breeze." The buildings were woven structures standing on poles or stilts.
Food and Mealtimes   "Morning, kind of a spongy custard and a little sweet. Evening, a gruel with milk in bowls. No utensils, wooden bowl." The mother was there at mealtimes, but no others.
Childhood Activities   "Some sport played with leather thongs attached to my right hand, like whipping them in the wind."
Mature-Life Activities   "We moved constantly, setting up camp, taking down camp. I was frightened lest we didn't move fast enough. Had to cover so much ground. Overwhelming feeling of fear, must constantly drive animals, sometimes over rough terrain, must hurry. No real emotions—all persons more or less equal."
Death   Died in his twenties. Time period chosen was 2000 B.C. The cause

of death was a fever. "I kissed my body goodbye. I had loved it so. It was strong and muscular and I loved it."

Karmic Connections   "One girl at work looks like a woman I was attracted to."

TRIP 2

Sex   Male as male
Place   Middle East, close to what now is eastern Iraq/Iran.
Appearance   Long gray-white hair and beard.
Dress   Sandals with open toes and loose-flowing robe. Wore a dhoti as a child.
Landscape and Terrain   "Desert in some spots; orchards in others. Small huts—no windows."
Food and Mealtimes   "Fruit juice made of different fruit—purple." Family was present.
Childhood Activities   "Shopping, holding to mother's skirt. Sculpting—chisel and rock."
Mature-Life Activities   "Writing; but by sculpting on slates, etching figures into stone, rather soft material."
Death   Died at age 79. Time period chosen was 2000 B.C. The cause of death was respiratory failure. The feelings about death: "Acceptance—waiting." The religious teaching was that we "come to God" after death. The spirit left the body as a spiral, and overlooked the scene of death. Daughter and family were there.
Karmic Connections   "Yes, with wife."

TRIP 2

Sex   Female as male
Place   Persia-Mesopotamia
Appearance   "Dark, oily, curly hair and large muscular hands."
Dress   Leather weskit and skirt. Coarse sandals.
Landscape and Terrain   "Hot, dry, dusty village or city, with adobe-type buildings."
Food and Mealtimes   Mutton, cooked, rather greasy. "Ate with fingers" from common clay pot.
Childhood Activities   "Active running, playing at fighting with sticks with other boys." Father was teaching reading. Wore homespun robe.
Mature-Life Activities   Slave overseer. Slaves were building a wall, making adobe bricks. "I was rough, tough, no compassion. Had compassion for wife, tender with her. She was unable to have a child."

Death Died at age 30 in 1970 B.C. The cause of death was a rock blow on the head. The feelings were grief at leaving wife. When the spirit left the body, "saw bloody head, big brawny body lying discarded in dirt."

Karmic Connections None mentioned.

TRIP 1

Sex Female as female

Place Palestine area

Appearance Coarse, black, long, thick, curly hair.

Dress Small sandals and togalike, coarse, natural-colored outer garment.

Landscape and Terrain "Desert, hot and humid." Open sky, patio or terrace with pillars around.

Food and Mealtimes "Grain, like rice; broth (flavored)." The eating utensil was a "scoop of bone that fits neatly in palm of left hand, also bread for scoop." A pottery bowl with a lip was used also.

Community Event "Men in courtyard area, going to a war."

Getting Supplies Grain was kept in a small storeroom in sacks, and baskets were used for carrying between storeroom and cooking place. The money used was "first, none, then polished stones for trading."

Death Died in 1492 B.C. at the age of 16. Murdered as she lay on a cot by a large, obese man. Feelings about death were "resignation." Feelings after death: "Bland. A little lost feeling but centered as a spirit."

TRIP 1

Sex Female as male

Place Greece

Appearance "Sore hands, rugged hands. Dirty dark hair."

Dress "Leather strap sandals. Itchy wool with leather tie-strap belt (like a short dress)."

Landscape and Terrain "Dry and hot. Barren and brushy hills." Buildings were adobe-looking clay, plain and dark inside.

Food and Mealtimes "Mutton soup with hard bread," eaten from wooden bowl with a spoon. A woman was stirring over kettle at fire.

Community Event "Fighting and stoning, hiding and running from enemy."

Getting Supplies The marketplace was lonely, with only a few buildings. He purchased a green vegetable that looked like a squash. He went to the market on foot and paid with a coin.

Death Died in 1447 B.C. at about age 30. "Stabbed in a fight, jumped from behind by a partly bald man (with a ponytail at top of head)." The feelings about death: "Didn't want to end this way."

TRIP 2

Sex Female as female
Place Judea
Appearance Dark medium-to-coarse wavy hair. Fair skin.
Dress Sandals and a long, loose rope belt.
Landscape and Terrain Near a river, with hills across the river. It was warm and somewhat barren.
Food and Mealtimes The food was meat, bread, and fruit. Parents and siblings were there.
Childhood Activities Sewing and playing outside with pets.
Mature-Life Activities Mother, wife, homemaker, weaving.
Death Died in thirties or forties. "Fell after some type of attack." She was sorry to leave her young children and grieving husband so early. "Believe in life hereafter."
Karmic Connections None mentioned.

TRIP 3

Sex Female as female
Place Toe of Italy
Appearance "Coarse curly dark hair, smooth dark hands."
Dress "Gray-white pleated tunic to mid-thigh. Rope-type sandals with rough leather soles."
Landscape and Terrain Desert. Arid, dry sand; but along a riverbank growth was green and lush.
Community Event "Some politically important person who was paid homage to—Pharaoh? high priest?—came to visit. I think to collect taxes."
Journey Made by water in a two-sailed reed or bamboo-type boat. "Only saw down a river, saw no destination, only water endlessly. Lots of palm trees and small settlements made up of straw and mud huts."
Religious Ceremony "Spring planting festival. Some type of grain." Wore a white tunic, heard gongs and bells. The feeling was "peaceful, joyous."
Death Died in 1200 B.C. of old age. The body was "old, wrinkled, yet still the body of a middle-aged woman; maybe died around 40." The cause of death: "Died in my sleep." The experience immediately after death was "peace, acceptance." The body was embalmed and wrapped

in linen, and buried in the sand. "My job was that of a scribe, wrote in symbols, pictures *but* not like hieroglyphics—seemed to be all mixed up—in Egypt, in Italy, and in Syria."

TRIP 3

Sex   Female as female

Place   Babylon

Appearance   Wavy hair arranged in bun on back of upper head.

Dress   Tunic, one piece with metal chain belt. Straw-soled shoes. Light-blue printed cloth over front of foot.

Landscape and Terrain   "Arid, pleasant, clear."

Community Event   "Meeting about impending invaders closing in towards us. Some folks upset. Most fairly confident that they'll never get near us (we have a very efficient force)."

Journey   Made by cart and horses on a *road*. "Just out tripping. The farmers and peasants are really impressed by our class (an illusion) and are very friendly—wish to hear about the center."

Religious Ceremony   "Like an astral projection exercise." Wore a white, longer tunic, with high belt. "One man speaking at first—sound/emotion impulses. The force of elemental energy—has sort of a sound experience—wind or underwater sound." The purpose was to "loosen our bonds."

Death   Died in forties of an accident: "Post fell in a tented market." The body was broken. It was carried off and burned after ceremony. The experience after death: "Slow release. Saw marketplace commotion about me and other injured person." "There was a thing that came into my head like dichy dichy, no date; a bit later, though, 700 B.C. came, but there was no dating system."

TRIP 2

Sex   Male as female

Place   Uncertain

Appearance   Long hair and fine, dark hands with somewhat rough palms. Skin tanned. Long nails on fingers.

Dress   Mostly bare feet, sometimes skins on feet. As an adult, sometimes naked. As a child, wrapped in skins or furs in winter, lighter skins in summer.

Landscape and Terrain   "Trees, rocks, mountains. Climate changes—cold winter; wet, warm summer. Days pleasant."

Food and Mealtimes   "Meat cooked on stick over open fire. No utensils."

Childhood Activities   "Playing in water, swimming, running naked." The skills learned were: making needles to sew skins, making thread from animal gut, preparing skins, and cooking meat. Also looking for edible roots and fruit.

Mature-Life Activities   "Love, security, my man keeps me well, happy life. I tend my man, water, food. I know his needs. Together we love, not knowing what 'love' is. Sex is total pleasure."

Death   Died "aged, but not old." Time period chosen was 500 B.C. "My man and I are walking together, a wild animal leaps for my man, I see it and scream, pushing him aside. I fall down over a bank. I don't want to leave my man. He is weeping, tired, hurts inside. Anger. I know I will be no more." The experience of leaving the body was "exciting physically and emotionally."

Karmic Connections   None mentioned.

TRIP 1

Sex   Male as male

Place   Somewhere on east coast of South Mexico or Central America

Appearance   Slender worn hands. Dark long hair, two braids. Yellow-brown skin; long, slender hairless feet.

Dress   "Sort of stylized, almost Egyptian-looking; no shirt; high wide leather or skin skirt with waist wrap."

Landscape and Terrain   "Warm/comfortable mild hills, just in from coast near river." The buildings were made of clay, wood, stone—some of them dug in caverns.

Food and Mealtimes   "Pasty corn mealish mush, eaten with pita-style bread/tortilla." The others eating were a "mate-type woman and an old, fat woman." The utensils were "my hands and the bread to scrape the black, polished clay bowl."

Community Event   A ceremony. Very intense, with other men participating.

Getting Supplies   "Going to an alkaline lake or something for *salt*." The method of travel was walking. "I just scooped it into a skin or cloth, then later into a pot. Very quiet/no people, very flat desert landscape, birds, bugs making noise. I just took what I needed—trade what I have for what I need."

Death   Death was at age 45 or 50. The year chosen was 500 B.C. At the time of death the date came as "year or period of the *Deer* or horse or some kind of four-legged animal." The cause of death: "Worn out." Feelings about death: "Comfort like a release or dissemination—

death felt fairly *organic.*" After death, there was a "familiarity with *lack of surrounding.*"

TRIP 1

Sex Male as male

Place Africa

Appearance "Long, silky, black thick hair. Large hands like feet." Feet were large, bare, hairy masculine, rough, gnarled, and grotesque. Body was naked, muscular, stocky, hard, hairy, with light-brown skin.

Dress None.

Landscape and Terrain "Clear clean air, gentle breeze. Flowers. Mountainous, plush green, hot, humid. Ocean, rocks, trees. Other caves."

Food and Mealtimes Eating at the same time were a woman, son, daughter, and an old woman. The food was "wild bird of some kind. Not anything I know now." The utensils were sticks and earthen pots.

Community Event "Sexual mating dance before fire—hot, passionate, excited for my wife-to-be—high."

Getting Supplies The method of travel was on foot. "Went to water—got green rocks. Exchanged rocks with a neighbor for fur skin. He lived other side of the valley in a cave."

Death Died at age 60 in 560 B.C. "while hunting with son. Large animal attacked me." Feelings about death: "Not suspecting, not important—accepted as normal course of events. Sad because son was sad." The feeling after death: "Nothingness—view body from above—out of body looking down on son and my body, sad but nothing else. One moment in body, next minute out and observing."

TRIP 1

Sex Male as male

Place Central Asia (southern Russia)

Appearance "Black, straight" hair, hands weathered. "Trader in utensils."

Dress "Wool robe; soft-leather pointed shoes."

Landscape and Terrain Central Asia, near Caspian Sea. Mountains with snow to the east. The buildings were adobe.

Food and Mealtimes "Lamb, olives, spices, alcoholic beverage (sweet)." The utensils were "greasy fingers, copper dish, pottery cup (no handle)." A helper stood to the right and a servant girl to the left.

Community Event "Temple ceremony; bright-red tunic, gold border. Human sacrifice. Relieved it's not me."

Getting Supplies Walking east to mountains with a donkey. The supplies purchased are copper and brass utensils from "kinsmen in mountain village." The money used is "gold (larger than a quarter) and crude copper."

Death Death was at age 57 in 493 B.C. "Something wrong with throat (growth?)." The feelings about death: "Life wasn't exciting, but I was basically good. Didn't hurt anybody. Looking at body, worn, but not worn out."

TRIP 1

Sex Female as female

Place Egypt

Appearance "Long shiny black hair." Delicate woman's hands.

Dress Brown sackcloth tunic with hood and rope tie around waist. Sandals, with crossed ties to the knees.

Landscape and Terrain "Sand desert, mountains (large hills in background), overcast, cool." Cold at first, then sunny. The buildings seen were pyramids.

Food and Mealtimes "Mealy-type food (bland). Utensil used was formed food like bread." Food was eaten from a clay bowl.

Community Event "I was a milkmaid with a yoke. It was a sunny, warm day. I was milking the goats on the hillside, listening to the ram's horn denoting the end of day—feeling free as a bird and excited about being with loved ones for dinner."

Getting Supplies Went to market on an animal, possibly a horse. The marketplace was outdoors, without buildings, but there was a light-green domed building in the background. Cloth was purchased with gold coins—small and round, with markings.

Death Death was at age 23 to 30 in 483 B.C. The cause of death was beheading, and the feeling about death was anxiety: "I developed a pain during the first part of the period chosen. The pain was in my heart, radiating through to my back (as if something was stuck through my body). I was a prisoner—a spy—my costume was a disguise, and I was found out. I was helping build something: the Great Pyramid?"

TRIP 1

Sex Male as male

Place Asia Minor—southern part near coast of Lydia.

Appearance "White skin, black hair, hairy arms, rough long fingers. Rough feet."

Dress Wool tunic with copper belt and sandals made of wood.

Landscape and Terrain "Open plains with background of hills, river, lakes with reeds, bushes. Tents made of tanned skins."

Food and Mealtimes Beans with chunks of lamb and barley eaten from wooden bowls. Bread is used as the eating utensil.

Community Event "A dancer is coming to town with a troupe. My wife is jealous." Heard bells and braying of donkeys.

Getting Supplies Went to market on a camel with a pack train of mules. The supplies purchased were bags of wheat. The purchase was made with "silver coins in leather pouch worn on waist—imprinted with woman's profile—had wreath around forehead."

Death Death was in 486 B.C., in mid-forties. The cause was a spear through the chest. Feelings about death: "Surprise, regret, nonacceptance, rebelliousness. My spirit felt deep regret at not appreciating the beauty of my body and its life."

10

LIFE FROM A.D. 25 to 1200

Life in A.D. 25

Ninety-seven of my subjects, or 9 percent of the total, went to a lifetime in the period around A.D. 25, the poorest of all the time periods, according to my data. In that period, only 3 percent of my subjects led an upper class life; 22 percent were artisans or merchants; and a full 75 percent were lower class. This distribution held for both sample group 1 and sample group 2, meaning that it was a consistent phenomenon when I repeated the study. I had expected to have some dramatic, glittering lives in ancient Rome if the past-life recall was based on fantasy. Instead, many of my subjects in Rome were very poor. In checking the history books, I learned that A.D. 25 was indeed a period of great poverty, especially in Rome.

The Rome of A.D. 25 is described by historians as being much like the New York City of 1977. The poor from many different areas flocked into Rome, the capital of the world at that time, where there was not only less trade than there had been in the earlier B.C. periods, according to my data, but also fewer people who were engaged in crafts or skilled occupations. In all the areas around the Mediterranean, from Egypt through the Near East to Greece, my subjects were poorer than they had been in the B.C.

periods. The history books do show that the period around the birth of Christ was a time of decayed civilizations in the Middle East and in Egypt, and the great conquests of Rome were due as much to the exhaustion of the earlier civilizations as to the skill of the Roman soldiers.

Death by violence was slightly higher in A.D. 25 than it had been in the earlier time periods, but the difference was not marked. Sixty-three percent of my subjects died of natural causes. However, some of these deaths were apparently due to starvation (I always list starvation deaths as natural because they are certainly not suicidal nor accidental). None of my subjects in A.D. 25 died in any formal battles, but a number of them reported being killed in small skirmishes. All in all, as I look at the regressions for A.D. 25, I feel that it wasn't a very good time to be alive.

The sex distribution for A.D. 25 is 49 percent male lives and 51 percent female.

Thirty percent of my subjects were in the Near East in A.D. 25. Of these, nine reported they were in the area of Israel or Palestine, and the remaining twenty-one were scattered through Saudi Arabia, Lebanon, and Mesopotamia. I had expected that many of my subjects would fantasize lives in which they saw Christ in A.D. 25. The literature of the occult strongly emphasizes past lives around the time of Christ, and if these past-life recalls were fantasy, I felt that such experiences would be reflected in my data. Actually, three subjects saw an image of Christ when I gave them a choice of this time period, but, as one of them reported, "I saw an image of Christ, but I realized that I wasn't Him. I wasn't anywhere around there." Another three subjects did report something related to Christ when I took them to an exciting event in A.D. 25. One said she was in a large crowd when Christ was crucified, another that she was watching Christ preach, while the third reported, "I'm with a group and they're saying that *He* is coming." She didn't specify who the "He" was, but as she capitalized the "H," I assumed she meant Christ. Altogether, these reports accounted for about 3 percent of the sample in A.D.

25, far fewer than I would have expected if past-life recall were fantasy.

The following sampling of data sheets report past-life experiences from around A.D. 25 through the first century A.D.

TRIP 1

Sex Female as male
Place Eastern Turkey or Middle East
Appearance Hands were slender and tan, feet light brown and slender.
Dress "Tan loose-fitting robe that felt like muslin." Sandals on feet.
Landscape and Terrain "Desert with mountains in distance. Overcast, but hot and dry." Grouped together are light-brown squarish buildings.
Food and Mealtimes "Something like stew. Only remember a brass ladle." Mother, father, and younger brother were also eating.
Community Event "A crowd going to see someone important."
Getting Supplies Walked to market to buy grain at food stalls. The money used was a brass coin about the size of a quarter.
Death Died in early twenties, in A.D. 36, of a fever. Feelings after death: "Release, looked down at the form wrapped in blankets."

TRIP 3

Sex Female as male
Place India, fairly close to river.
Appearance Closely cropped hair, nearly shaved. Very slender feet.
Dress White, loose garment, barefooted. As a boy, wore a hat similar to Shriners'.
Landscape and Terrain None mentioned. House had woven matting.
Community Event "Some great man coming through the village."
Journey The journey was made "on back of an elephant, a pleasant journey to the river for supplies." They passed jungle-type greenery, and he had pleasant conversations with his father.
Religious Ceremony "Praying for prosperous season (plants)." They were dressed in white. The sound "O-ma" was repeated many times. "I had a great belief or desire to believe."
Death Died as an old man in A.D. 43. The body was wrapped in white cloth and burned. The body was very skinny, and death was apparently cause from old age. The feeling after death: "I was going to be judged."
Karmic Connections None specified

TRIP 1

Sex Female as male

Place Southern Italy, southeast.

Appearance Hair smooth, fine and short to shoulders. Hands square and capable.

Dress Leather-type sandals enclosing feet thoroughly. A brown tunic with leather-type belt. Material was rough serge.

Landscape and Terrain "Dry, harsh, barren, rolling mountains in distance. Hot and dry." The buildings "seem like white slab."

Food and Mealtimes Pastelike food and fruit, eaten with wooden spoon from wooden plates. "Old grandfather to right. Not so clear—mother and young girl (sister)."

Community Event "Fighting like a sports event, clashing of metal, lots of dust."

Getting Supplies Went to market with donkey and cart to purchase sacks of grain. There was a cool building in which the grain was kept. Paid for with silver coins taken from a pouch hung from his waist.

Death Died at age 40. Buried under stones in an avalanche, in A.D. 49. After death, "I pull out of body. Very blue colors everywhere."

TRIP 1

Sex Female as male

Place Jerusalem?

Appearance Coarse brown hair streaked with blond. Hands were large— a worker's hands, yet artistic and fine. Large brown feet, flat.

Dress Loosely draped, cream-neutral in color; rough, yet a fine material and weave. Sandals.

Landscape and Terrain Hot, warm. A blue mountain in the distance with water below it. Cultivated green stalks in foreground. White clay buildings.

Food and Mealtimes Mushy maize, brown grain bread. "I eat with my hands at a low table. Corn dish has sweet taste." The plate is "heavyish, sturdy, hard; perhaps hard-baked clay on metal."

Community Event "Race with donkeys and carts; I am gambling with other men. I want to win; when 18, I drove them myself." Wore scarlet-and-white striped tunic for the special occasion.

Getting Supplies The marketplace is large, with many people. "It's a somewhat hard time, little water, but people are used to it." Walked next to donkey which carried jugs for water. The supplies purchased were water, which was paid for with a round coin, carried in a leather pouch at the waist. "The coin had a picture of man's helmeted head, numbers on it like CV."

Death   Died at age 82–83 in A.D. 80. "I am an old man—heart, liver." The feelings about death: "I am sorry to leave, but philosophical. My brother-in-law is at my side. My sister married a good boy." After death the feelings were: "Sorrow—I liked that old man; but no feeling of tragedy. Tears ran down my cheeks."

TRIP 1

Sex   Male as male
Place   Eastern coast of Italy
Appearance   None mentioned.
Dress   Wooden shoes, baggy pants, and hat.
Landscape and Terrain   "Cobblestone village, stone overpass." Buildings were of stone.
Food and Mealtimes   Kind of a thick soup, "like *really* thick split pea soup." Ate with wooden spoon, and there was one other person around.
Community Event   Could not see. "Lots of high-energy people."
Getting supplies   Went on foot to a wood and stone marketplace. Wooden beads were purchased with a brass-colored coin about the size of a large fifty-cent piece.
Death   Died in A.D. 89 of old age. The feeling after death: "Good—light— spreading out."

TRIP 3

Sex   Female as male
Place   Mideast, south of Israel and Egypt on eastern side.
Appearance   Black hair, beard; thick hands.
Dress   Short skirt, tunic, sandals.
Landscape and Terrain   "Dry, arid, flat, but with rocky cliffs and the wide, lazy river."
Community Event   "The arresting of Jesus' followers. Man speaking about how they should not be allowed to come to the city and have meetings."
Journey   The journey was from Bar-A-Tek to Nazareth by horse. It was a long journey, and on the way saw "hills, small village, deep valley or cavern."
Religious Ceremony   "Later years. A group of Christians in a small room." Their dress was simple brown clothing. The song sung was something like "Ra-ma, Neu-tee—Say-Toe-La-Ma-Ain Toe—Ca bra entu mesa." The purpose of the ceremony was "worship of personal connection to

spirit world." He was "uncomfortable, because I never did it before, but I felt safe and not threatened."

Death   Died at age 65–70 in A.D. 144. The cause of death was old age, and the body was thin, quiet, empty. The experience after death was "spinning forward, light circling forward and then a feeling of free tumbling and delightful playing." The body was "wrapped in a blanket on a table." "People came to put their hands on me."

Karmic Connections   None specified.

Life in A.D. 400

Sixty of my subjects went to the A.D. 400 time period, comprising 6 percent of the total sample. In distribution, the upper class was only 3 percent of the population in A.D. 400, the middle class 20 percent, and the lower class 77 percent. These data are comparable to the figures for the upper class percentage in A.D. 25; A.D. 400 was again a depressed period as far as culture and civilization were concerned. There were few artisans or tradesmen, and most people were simply trying to survive through subsistence farming. In A.D. 400 the figure for death by violence was 20 percent; most of these deaths occurred in raids or small wars. Fully 10 percent of the sample in A.D. 400 did not experience their deaths. The male/female ratio in that period was 47 percent male and 53 percent female.

Eighteen percent of my sample found themselves in the Near East in A.D. 400. Most of these subjects were in the eastern regions, from Turkey to Lebanon; only one was in Palestine. Most of the lives described were very simple. However, there were two upper class lives in the Near East, which indicates that this area had a rich civilization. There were no wealthy people among the European samples.

The following reports cover past-life regressions up to around A.D. 400.

TRIP 2

Sex   Female as male
Place   Southwestern Canada or northeastern China
Appearance   "Long, long fingernails. Mongolian—Indian."

Dress None specified.

Landscape and Terrain Trees, cool, arid. Thatched A-frame dwellings with woven walls.

Food and Mealtimes Eating rice with fingers, and some substance rolled in leaves. Saw the smiling face of a round, young, Eskimo-looking woman.

Childhood Activities "Played marbles in dirt. Tied spearhead to stick with thin rope."

Mature-Life Activities "Hunting, climbing, worshiping, maybe a medicine man or something." Had images of trying to look fierce and frightening in tribal costume.

Death Died in his thirties. Cause of death was falling from a high place onto rock. "Maybe I was pushed, landed on my back." The religious teaching was that "things went on." When the spirit left the body, "Just could see body, long black hair lying neatly in place all around head." She was puzzled about the time. "I tried for 400 A.D., but am unsure of where I ended up."

Karmic Connections None specified.

TRIP 2

Sex Female as male

Place Southern Europe, along the Mediterranean. "Lived in town right by the water."

Appearance "Dark, fine, curly, soft, short hair. Muscular and strong hands. Muscular man's feet." Light complexion.

Dress "Leather with metal belt."

Landscape and Terrain He was on a ship with wood planks. "Image of ship in storm." The buildings flashed on were a childhood home, emotionally warm, cozy, and comfortable.

Food and Mealtimes Fish, olive oil. "My mother, she was young, pretty smile on her face."

Childhood Activities "Playing along canals or near waterfront. Something to do with rope."

Mature-Life Activities Working on the ship, climbing the mast, looking at the sunset. "Calm water, warm evening on the Mediterranean."

Death Died at age 70–80. Time period chosen was A.D. 400. The cause of death was old age, but there was some pain in the chest and side. The feelings about death were calm, peaceful. "Well-lived life, content with it but no outstanding accomplishment."

Karmic Connections "None except a strong connection with my mother in that life. Mother was very happy with me. I seemed to be her only child and she was proud of me and emotionally close. Sense of her not being much older than me."

TRIP 2

Sex Female as male

Place Somewhere on the American continent

Appearance Black, straight, oily hair and dark, reddish skin.

Dress Bare feet, skins and hides around ankles; light leather and heavier fur pieces on rest of body.

Landscape and Terrain "Rocky terrain, bushes abundant, sparse but large trees; dry." No buildings were in sight.

Food and Mealtimes "Dried fish and nuts or berries. No family feeling, but a few adults and children around fire pit."

Childhood Activities Making weapons, grinding stones on stone to make them sharp. Dancing in an initiation rite.

Mature-Life Activities "Gathering herbs or plants, catching fish in a stream by hand. Tutoring or raising a son to follow my skill."

Death Died at age 40 from falling off a cliff or down on some rocks. The feeling about death was one of surrender, and the religious teaching had been one of nature worship rather than people worship. He felt it was useless to resist death and found it a welcome release. The time period chosen was A.D. 400, but he said the "number 9 kept popping up. Just the number 9," when asked about the time of death.

Karmic Connections None mentioned.

TRIP 2

Sex Female as male

Place Africa

Appearance Hair was long, black, with strands of gray, and curly. Hands were well shaped, strong, and slender.

Dress "Crude leather sandals. Coarse, dark-brown, sleeveless short tunic." As a child, had rope tied at waist.

Landscape and Terrain Desert in Africa, Sahara—western area; dry, terribly hot sand dunes, but walked on crunchy surface, which was noisy and hot underfoot. Saw the remainder of a stone and plaster caravanserai, fallen apart and abandoned. "Very little shade."

Food and Mealtimes "Stew, lots of big pieces of meat, vegetables, broth. Good! Unleavened bread." Ate with mother and father.

Childhood Activities "Playing with a ball-like object outside. Very happy." The skill learned was jewelry making.

Mature-Life Activities "A skilled jeweler. This is an intense, intelligent man. Unfulfilled, unhappy, has many longings. A cultured household, but not rich. Very modest, dedicated people." "This image flashed *very strong.* Tramping across the desert hurriedly, two long lines of us, driven on by guards on camels. Could feel the heat, see a bare, hairy left leg and hear the crunch of the harsh surface of the desert. Feeling was of forcing myself to go on regardless of pain and heat. Staring numbly ahead."

Death   Died at age 36 from exhaustion and then "a deliberate spear thrust, during a forced march across the desert as a prisoner." "Died within sight of a desert city." At death he was determined to live on, and the religious teaching was Christian. "Death and the spirit leaving came at the same moment. Felt fiercely determined to *go on.* When I saw my spirit going out and up, it was okay. Triumphant." Date of death was A.D. 415.

Karmic Connection   Teacher then was father now and mother then is mother now.

TRIP 2

Sex   Male as male

Place   Middle of Nile region

Appearance   Stringy black hair.

Dress   No shoes, stiff short pants.

Landscape and Terrain   Stone white buildings, a slight incline, a river, moderate climate.

Food and Mealtimes   Food was bitter, sproutlike and crunchy, moist. Ate in a family circle.

Childhood Activities   "Spear throwing at disc, and pottery making."

Mature-Life Activities   "Plow and plant most of the time."

Death   Died at age 87 in AD. 425. Cause of death was unknown, and the feeling was one of rest. When the spirit left the body, he felt a shaft of white leaving the top of the head. "It was a boring lifetime."

Karmic Connections   None specified.

TRIP 2

Sex   Male as male

Place   Northern Germany, Black Forest.

Appearance   Hair was thick, dark, and matted. Strong, large, gnarled hands.

Dress   Wore furs, a hat with horns, and sandals, which were roughly made and tight.

Landscape and Terrain   Climate was cool, northern temperate. It was the end of winter and still cold. He saw a tent with a huge pole in the center—dark, brownish, drab in color—with an opening at the top.

Food and Mealtimes Very uncooked meat—torn from the cooked animal. There were a lot of people around, all related, including an older bearded man and a shy lady—a cousin.

Childhood Activities A man was teaching. "My father—killed him for it later." He learned archery, but was "very clumsy and others laughed." He was the worst one. He hated all the people around him, who were all related to him.

Mature-Life Activities "War. Charging on a hillside with my tribe against another tribe. Led the way and won."

Death He died at age 45 and was roasted alive face down by his enemies after being wounded to exhaustion. "Didn't move. I wanted to show my enemies my strength, and so I stopped the glee at my death by dying so stoically that they killed me. A woman was chosen to relieve my pain as a gesture of appreciation for a great warrior." He had no religious teaching other than the worship of some pagan gods. The spirit leaving the body freed him from the responsibility of leading people. Date of death was 493.

Karmic Connections "Cousin woman was my mother, I think."

Life in A.D. 800

Sixty-eight subjects, or 6 percent of the total sample, experienced past lives in the A.D. 800 time period. Fifty percent of these lives were lived as males and 50 percent as females. The upper, middle, and lower class figures are much the same as in A.D. 400: 2 percent upper class, 28 percent middle class, and 71 percent lower class. Natural deaths accounted for 65 percent of the sample, and there were 24 percent accidental and 11 percent violent deaths.

Slightly more middle class lives were lived in this time period, indicating that civilization, though still at a low point, was moving upward from where it had been in the A.D. 25 and A.D. 400 time periods. The percentage of subjects in the Near East was decreasing rapidly and formed only 6 percent of the total sample in A.D. 800.

The following reports describe lives in the time period from A.D. 500 to A.D. 900.

TRIP 3

Sex Female as male

Place West border of Japan

Appearance "Smooth, clean fingernails, not used to manual labor; very coarse black hair, almost shoulder length."

Dress "Short, pleated light-brown skirt, looked like large rows of turquoise." Sandals on feet.

Landscape and Terrain "Tilled crops; looked like nice leafy ones, all neat in rows."

Community Event "Some elders sitting in middle; others all around in semicircle. I was in audience; courtlike setup, talking about crops, fertilizer, etc. All men in audience. All shook hands and were happy at end of meeting."

Journey Made on foot with packs on back, in company with three or four other young men. The journey was made to a hotel room, where there were cots and we slept overnight. The room was sparsely furnished, with a window. "We slept there overnight and looked at stars."

Religious Ceremony "I was dancing up in front of others with few clothes on but long piece of cloth on back. I was rain leader." He heard a chant of four syllables, all in unison. The purpose of the ceremony was "to get rain." His feelings were that "all of us were in unison; good feeling."

Death Death came at age 25 or 30, in A.D. 671. He was stoned to death by a large number of people because there was no rain. The body was "all bloody." Immediately after death, he "knew it was necessary." The body was piled with a little dirt and then burned. "Many people around. They clapped, part of custom."

Karmic Connections "A young male friend was my father in this life."

TRIP 3

Sex Female as female

Place Turkey (Central Asia)

Appearance "Sturdy, worker type, long black hair."

Dress Sandals, long skirt, cape of heavy cotton and wool.

Landscape and Terrain "Hot in summer, cold in winter. Desert area. Route between Turkey and Afghanistan." Part of a nomadic group traveling across the desert.

Community Event "We would attend meetings of other nomadic groups. Lots of tents and Oriental rugs in tents."

Journey "By camel, mule, and horse caravan. Trips back and forth from Turkey to Afghanistan. I was part of a large group, a large nomadic tribe of merchants who traveled back and forth across the trade routes, buying and selling merchandise. We stayed in tents at night and traveled during the day. I was a very capable 40-year-old mother and business woman, who spent her life on the trade routes between Turkey and Afghanistan."

Religious Ceremony   "A baptism of some kind—a new baby." The purpose was to welcome a new child into the tribe. "Very warm and traditional." Everyone wore long capes and hoods, "all sitting around inside our permanent home, where the older members stay year round."

Death   Died at about age 70 in A.D. 746. The cause of death was "old age." The body was cremated and buried in the sands of the desert.

Karmic Connections   None mentioned.

TRIP 2

Sex   Female as male

Place   Persia

Appearance   Turban.

Dress   Loose, muslin-wrapped shirt/shorts; barefoot, with white powder dust on feet.

Landscape and Terrain   A fertile, warm, green climate, and a stone building with thick walls and steps. There are paintings on the walls.

Food and Mealtimes   Mother and father were there, and the food was rice, spicy.

Childhood Activities   Painting a vase at about 12 years of age.

Mature-Life Activities   Painting in a temple; on the floor was a mat. There was a peaceful garden outside.

Death   Died at age 24. Cause of death was a "spear in my forehead." "I was not ready but not scared." The religious teaching was that he was a priest or a "wise" man who was to travel to place on the other side. When the spirit left the body it was "flowing—rippling outward." Death was in 892.

Karmic Connections   "Yes, my wife is a woman I know now who has been my teacher for two years. When I saw the woman (karmic connection), my body rippled with shivers, warm chills."

Life in A.D. 1200

One hundred seven, or 10 percent of my sample, experienced lives in 1200. Fifty-four percent of these lived lives as men, and 46 percent as females. The upper class formed 6 percent of the sample of both the first group and the replication study, the middle class 28 percent of all the subjects, and the lower class 74 percent. The percentage of violent deaths went down in 1200, indicating that more civilized lives were being experienced by my subjects at this time as compared to the Dark Ages. Just as the middle class increased from 20 to 28 percent of the sample, so the percentage of natural deaths went up to 58 percent. There was some evidence of more deaths in war, and twenty-six subjects experienced death in warfare. Some of these deaths appear to have occurred in the Crusades, but others apparently resulted from local skirmishes among European dukes and lords.

Fourteen, or 10 percent, of my subjects in 1200 went to the Near East. Life in the Near East seems to have been more poverty-stricken in 1200 than it had been in the A.D. 400 and A.D. 800 time periods. The data sheets give a varied picture of lives in medieval times.

TRIP 2

Sex Female as female

Place None specified

Appearance Calloused misshapen feet, dirty. Black, coarse, unkempt hair with cloth around the head.

Dress Coarse cloth dress, baggy, drab, no shoes.

Landscape and Terrain "Warm—by wide, dirty river." Sandstone buildings and a cobblestone street.

Food and Mealtimes Shared a rolled pancake filled with meat with three brothers and mother. Hungry. So concerned with food that everything else seemed unimportant.

Childhood Activities "Playing with other children, balancing on a fallen log." At age 5, splashing naked in water of river.

Mature-Life Activities "Mother of three children. No husband present." Caring for children, cooking, washing clothes.

Death Died at age 50+. "Smothered in mud, trampled by mob" seeking food. A time of terrible famine. "Glad life is finally over." She saw a frail, emaciated body, and heaved a sigh of relief. "Hunger was very real." The time period chosen was A.D. 1200.

Karmic Connections None specified.

TRIP 3

Sex Female as female

Place Kyoto, Japan.

Appearance "Have smooth, heavy, silky" hair and delicate hands.

Dress "Long, shiny, turquoise fabric with cummerbund (obi?)" On her feet she wore slippers with stockings, "strappings from slippers up socks."

Landscape and Terrain "Fall climate, crisp weather, mountains in the background."

Community Event "Harvest festival. I was feeling a little removed and would rather have been participating in a tea ceremony."

Journey An animal pulled a cart from the home village to a temple. Mountains were in the background.

Religious Ceremony A ceremony for the good harvest. "It was exactly where I wanted to be. The ceremony was spiritually beautiful. There was a chalice from which we drank a grapelike drink with some bitter taste to it. The chalice was marked with the design of a bird from which emanated rays. Just above the bird was a circle, which could have been the sun." There were "tinkling sounds, like bells and some high-pitched other sounds and chanting." She wore a full gown of something like silk, which she saw in colors.

Death Died in 1092 of apparent poisoning, "crumpling on the street, clutching my abdomen." The body was disposed of by cremation.

Karmic Connections None mentioned.

TRIP 2

Sex Male as male

Place Somewhere in western U.S. Mountain surrounded by plains.

Appearance "Long straight black hair, tanned skin; very, very healthy."

Dress Loin cloth, bare feet.

Landscape and Terrain Like California, or western U.S., with pleasant weather. No buildings in sight.

Food and Mealtimes "Strips of dried meats and fruits. Adequate. Food not important." Twenty or thirty families lived there. He ate with seven or eight others.

Childhood Activities "Learning to make tools, drilling holes in stone, like for pipe."

Mature-Life Activities "Moved to mountain with my lady. Gradually joined by friends in spiritual community. Small group, living like commune. We built conical 'tepees.'"

Death Died at age 35. "Fell in mountains while climbing. Rocks crumbled under my hands and I slid down feet first, facing mountain." Death was "no big deal." The transition to death was imperceptible. While still sliding, he was no longer in his body; "just lifted away from mountain." The time period chosen was A.D. 1200.

Karmic Connections "Had teacher with white hair, super-intense face. Very wise, and knew him in other lives." He noticed a woman who was the same in all lives.

TRIP 2

Sex Female as male

Place North of England. Hexham Abbey.

Appearance Body lean, spare, gaunt, tall. "Tonsure, grizzled otherwise."

Dress He wore sandals and had dirty feet. "Coarse brown monk's robe, rope girdle, hair shirt prickled."

Landscape and Terrain Pastoral, village. "I lived in abbey," which was partially built. Wooden farm buildings also seen.

Food and Mealtimes Turnips, very sharp and yellow. Father and others were there. "I felt unimportant."

Childhood Activities He was looking after animals, and wearing a rough tunic with leggings of cloth. At 17, "wanted to withdraw, be a monk."

Mature-Life Activities "In abbey I also tend the animals. Life is hard. Pray at regular intervals. Coming down the night stairs for first prayers of the day. Cold, bleak. I hear the chanting."

Death He died at age 61 in A.D. 1225 of a growth in the intestines. "Life was hard—painful—so is death." The religious teaching was "grim, hell, damnation." The experience of the spirit leaving the body was one of relief. "I gaze at body—it has been well worn."

Karmic Connections "Animals—no feel for connection with people; was pulled here—have had real experience at this particular abbey. Strong feeling while sitting on the night stairs that I'd been there before as a monk."

TRIP 2

Sex Female as female

Place Somewhere in Middle East in a European-type castle. Perhaps in Turkey.

Appearance "Fine slender feet." Long, smooth, not-quite-black hair, but dark. Hands were delicate, sensitive.

Dress "Thin leather sandals, flowing light gown."

Landscape and Terrain   Countryside, mild climate with farms, low hills. A castle and its village.

Food and Mealtimes   A group was eating; "sort of family."

Childhood Activities   "Very sheltered—learned spinning thread and sewing, etc."

Mature-Life Activities   "Walk around. I basically spent all my time within the castle, no responsibilities. Sometimes entertained by people, but not usually."

Death   "Died in my twenties." Cause of death was suicide. "I just wanted out." Wished for some religious training, but had had none. "After leaving that body, I just misted away and so did that whole consciousness." Date of death was 1297.

Karmic Connections   A man she was in love with in that lifetime is a woman she sees sometimes in this life and has some trouble with.

TRIP 2

Sex   Female as female

Place   Judea

Appearance   Dark medium-to-coarse wavy hair, fair skin.

Dress   Long and loose, with rope belt.

Landscape and Terrain   Warm and somewhat barren; near river, hills visible across river.

Food and Mealtimes   Meat, bread, fruit. Parents and siblings present.

Childhood Activities   Sing, play small harp.

Mature-Life Activities   Mother, wife, homemaker, weaving.

Death   Died in thirties or forties, falling down after some kind of attack. Was sorry to leave young children and grieving husband so early. Time was about 1300. Religious teaching taught belief in life hereafter.

11

LIVES FROM 1500 TO THE TWENTIETH CENTURY

Life in A.D. 1500

One hundred thirty-eight of my subjects, or 13 percent of the sample, went to lifetimes lived in the 1500s, as compared to 10 percent that had gone to 1200 and 6 percent to 800. This means that the population more than doubled from A.D. 800 to A.D. 1500. In this time period, 51 percent of my subjects had male lives, 49 percent female lives. The society seemed more civilized in 1500 than it had been in 1200; 8 percent of my sample belonged to the upper class, 30 percent to the middle class, and 62 percent to the lower class. In 1500, my subjects were more likely than before to be artisans, craftsmen, or people using a skill in a civilized context. Most of the lives were still simple; people lived off the land, and dressed and ate modestly. The causes of death in 1500 were 62 percent natural, an increase of 6 percent over the 1200s. There were correspondingly fewer violent deaths, 19 percent compared to 24 percent in 1200. Life was more settled and there appeared to be less danger from marauding bands or local wars. I thought I might get a lot of sailors in 1500, because that is our culture's image of a major activity at that time, but only six subjects reported being on ships or involved in any way in exploration, which is less than 3 percent of the sample in this time period.

The fact that only 7 percent of my subjects went to the Near East in 1500 indicates a steady decrease of subjects in the Near East since the high point for reported lives in that area in A.D. 25. Six of the subjects in the Near East were wearing rough burlap robes, as they had done in earlier time periods there. However, one Near Eastern life showed "a rough skirt with a bare top," suggesting a different dress style. This mode was reported near the Black Sea, which would reflect a nomadic life in the Caucasus region rather than a life in the populated regions of the Near East. In Mesopotamia in 1500, the culture was clearly more typical of the Ottoman Empire.

By 1500, most of these past-life regressions were experienced in both southern and northern Europe. The people who dressed well were a small percentage of the total; most of my subjects wore a longer variation of the tunics seen in the A.D. 1200 period. Men were beginning to wear trousers, and among the male subjects trousers outnumbered robes in my sample by three to one.

Six percent of my subjects went to South America in 1500. Three of them seemed to be in the Andes region of Peru and the other three led primitive lives scattered over other parts of the continent.

Only three subjects in my sample were in North America in 1500. Two of these lived lives as Indians, but the third was apparently my first reported lifetime of a Caucasian in the North American continent.

Three subjects had lives in Africa in 1500. One of these, a middle-class life in Egypt, had a dress style more typical of dress in the Moslem countries than of the Egyptian costumes described in the B.C. periods. The buildings were much the same, but the life style was more lavish than that described earlier.

The following reports describe regressions around the 1500 period.

TRIP 3

Sex Female as male
Place South America—Peru.
Appearance Black, coarse hair. Small child's hands.
Dress "A bright scarf tied around head (not under chin) as a child. Earring. Ponchos—brightly colored."
Landscape and Terrain Very cold. Valleys, mountains with snow.
Community Event "Lots of bells and jingling sound, watching brightly colored costumes, men bearing a litter—a sacrifice? Felt OK about it, a little sadness."
Journey Made on foot and by llama from the village to a mountain retreat. Observations on the journey: "The village getting farther away, the mountains and valleys, the llama being very docile."
Religious Ceremony "My journey was some kind of puberty rite. A meditation thing in the mountains." The sounds were bells, rattles, jingling sounds like thousands of metal things in rhythmical pattern. The purpose of the ceremony was entry into manhood. Feelings were "exhilaration, looking forward, taking all feelings in."
Death Died at age 70. The time period chosen was 1500. The body was very aged, costumed on a raised bier. The body was cremated.

TRIP 1

Sex Female as male
Place Normandy
Appearance "Blond, rough, medium sized, hairy, calloused."
Dress Rough knight's costume, silver or gray, like the undergarments of a knight's uniform. The shoes were silver smooth and rounded, possibly with spurs.
Landscape and Terrain "Trees, river, lush and cool." There is a castle with metal-covered round or conical top with flag. Other stone buildings.
Food and Mealtimes "Noodles, clear, leafy vegetables, hunk of meat." Food is served on plain pewter plates with a two-tined fork.
Community Event "Knights on horseback running toward one another with long metal poles. Tournament like the days of King Arthur, dogs on leash held by a woman."
Getting Supplies Went to market in wooden cart drawn by horses to buy coarse grain flour. The marketplace looked like a "western ghost town." The money used showed a crown on one side and three leaves on the other.

Death   Died at age 84 of natural causes. The feelings about death were: "Peaceful, light rising sensation, ready, tired, misery, alone." The time period chosen was 1500.

TRIP 1

Sex   Female as female

Place   Holland (Amsterdam?)

Appearance   Dark, coarse hair; plain working hands.

Dress   "Sturdy, worn-thin dark dress; white apron; linen cap, lace edging. Wooden shoes, old, bound to feet with cloth strips."

Landscape and Terrain   "Village in a plateau. Hills around. Warm, dry climate. Wooden market stalls, wooden houses."

Food and Mealtimes   "Bread, greens, red fruit like plums or tomatoes, beans." Ate from clay bowls with wooden spoons. Husband and son were also eating.

Community Event   "Circus comes to town. Horse-pulled carts filled with jesters, acrobats, pranksters. They flirt with me in front of the other spectators. I am flattered and embarrassed. I see myself as a plain, somewhat martyred woman."

Getting Supplies   Went to market on foot or in horse-drawn wooden carts. The supplies purchased were beans and red fruit like plums. The marketplace consisted of wooden stalls with carts of foods. Stalls were separated by cloth curtains. The money used was gold coins the size of a half dollar, with a face on one side and a tree on the other.

Death   Died in her eighties in A.D. 1589, of old age. The feeling about death was one of "acceptance—felt like it was time, resignation." The feelings after death were: "Relief—looked back on her and felt she'd missed a lot of joy in life."

TRIP 3

Sex   Female as female

Place   Southern Asia

Appearance   Hands had light-brown fingers, well-formed, meticulously manicured. Fine, soft hair. Compact feet, well manicured.

Dress   "Light-yellow sarong-type dress. Simple sandals."

Landscape and Terrain   Mountains; gentle jungle terrain.

Community Event   " 'Mother' overseeing temple/convent. Very gentle woman. She loved me very much—unconditionally. Straw on floor and walls, painted ceilings."

Journey "Countryside—aware of folks coming to temple for healing by the women." The journey was made sitting on top of hay in a two-wheeled wagon.

Religious Ceremony "Movement with lights. People in a long line holding objects and light over their heads. Spring or Birth Celebration." Felt light and serenely happy.

Death The time chosen was 1600. Died in late thirties. Cause of death was some form of illness with a fever. Experienced "release only" after death.

Life in 1700

By the 1700s life had improved for my subjects in most parts of the world, especially in Europe, where elaborate clothes were worn and cities had become nearly as populous as the countryside. Interestingly, for the first time there was an abundance of females: 52 percent, in comparison to 48 percent males. The upper class was represented by 10 percent of my subjects in 1700. Thirty percent of my subjects in 1700 were middle class, but a majority, 60 percent, were still classified as lower class. Cause of death varied from earlier time periods, but only by a few percentage points. More people died a natural death—64 percent—than in earlier time periods. The percent of violent deaths was 16 percent, and accidental death 17 percent.

Only 12 percent of my sample was in the Near East in 1700. Of these, one subject was a European living in Turkey. It is interesting to note that I begin to get a smattering of Europeans in distant parts of the world in the 1700s, as European countries colonize other continents. Sixty-three percent of my subjects were in Mediterranean Europe and northern Europe in the 1700s. In 1700, for the first time, a sizable number (21 percent) of my subjects were in North America. They represented three races: Caucasian, black, and American Indian. Four percent of my subjects went to South America, and, again, those who were Caucasians constituted evidence of white colonialism in that part of the world.

The sampling of reports that follow depict life in 1700.

TRIP 2

Sex   Female as male
Place   Turkey—Mersin—Blue Ocean.
Appearance   Black, curly, soft hair; small hands and feet. A boy.
Dress   Sandals, blue toga.
Landscape and Terrain   Sandy, rocky with green hills. The climate was sunny and warm. There was a large building with white columns, in ruins.
Food and Mealtimes   "Something sweet and sticky." Many friends were there and a baldheaded father.
Childhood Activities   "Playing with stick and a rock with friends. Making jewelry."
Mature-Life Activities   "Teacher. Cutting into stone tablet with chisel. Could see children—all boys—small, listening intently."
Death   Died at age 23 in A.D. 1715. Death was caused by being run over by a chariot. The feelings about death: "Anger—done on purpose by 'friend.' " Can't remember religious teaching, but had something to do with Olympia. The experience on leaving the body: "Regretful but happy."
Karmic Connections   "Best friend, then male, is [female] friend in this life. Other 'friend' killed me."

TRIP 1

Sex   Male as male
Place   North coast of Mediterranean
Appearance   "Large hands, dark hair on them, with one ring. Blond hair."
Dress   "Lavender pants that came below knee. Medium-rough material, silk, flowing white shirt. Low leather shoes, white stockings, appeared to be a gold buckle on shoes."
Landscape and Terrain   "On board sailing the vessel. In port, warm climate. Felt Mediterranean." Saw mostly two-story buildings. "Several on street across from where ship was tied up—gray slate roofs."
Food and Mealtimes   "Some sort of meat with brown sauce." Food was eaten from a shallow bowl with a three-pronged fork.
Community Event   "Some sort of celebration—not sure of meaning."
Getting Supplies   The method of going for supplies was by walking. The marketplace was a large mercantile center—quiet except for the outside noises of wagons and horses going by. Rice and dry goods were purchased with paper money, brown in color, and several large gold or copper coins.

Death Died at age 35 from a sword wound in a duel. The date of death was 1725. There was no fear of death. Feelings after death: "Freedom—spirit floated free—dark but calm and excited at the same time."

TRIP 1

Sex Male as female
Place England—West Chester.
Appearance "Very white long fingers."
Dress "Leather shoes, black. Soft striped black-and-white blouse with a large, very large collar. Lace around the collar. Full, soft skirt. Lots of undergarments." She wore a gold ring with a wide band.
Landscape and Terrain "Rolling hills, lots of green grass and trees. From my window I could see a group of thatched roofed buildings . . . maybe a barn or grain house."
Food and Mealtimes "Roast beef . . . very spicy." The food was eaten from a light-blue eight-sided plate. A man, another woman, a child, and a brother were also eating.
Community Event None mentioned.
Getting Supplies The method of travel to marked was a buggy or coach. The supplies purchased were blue satin material and thread. The destination was a small store with lots of small windows. "The name 'Warsaw' was written in gold leaf on the window." The supplies were purchased with gold coins with "a man's head on it."
Death The date of death was June 12, 1726, at age 26. The cause of death was a fall from a horse. Feelings about death: "Jason is going to feel so bad!" Feelings after death: "Sorry that I had not been more careful."

TRIP 3

Sex Male as female
Place Ceylon, India.
Appearance Black hair, brown hands.
Dress Wood sandals, very colorful short gown over long gown.
Landscape and Terrain "Hills and flatland, jungle, ocean, hot, muggy, lots of rain."
Community Event Many religious festivals.
Journey Made by horse or burro from Ceylon to Darjeeling by way of the Ganges and Benares, then on into the mountains.
Religious Ceremony Wore a wraparound cloth and was a musician. Fol-

lower of Rama. The purpose of the ceremony had something to do with Kali.

Death Died at age 48 from a fever. The body was paunchy and the hair gray at the temples. It was cremated. Date of death was 1746.

Karmic Connections Music.

TRIP 1

Sex Male as male

Place South Pacific Islands

Appearance Bald or shaven head. Caucasian; dark and hairy, with a mustache.

Dress "Baggy pants, striped shirt, stocking cap. Hard shoes, comfortable, not boots."

Landscape and Terrain "At sea, sunny, warm, light cooling breeze, peaceful." Could see the deckhouse.

Food and Mealtimes "Hard, salty meat. Drink, strong taste, thick." Food was eaten from deep plates eight to nine inches in diameter. A white-haired old man was eating quietly nearby; also another unhappy, suspicious man, whom "I tolerate."

Community Event "Natives canoeing to our ship. We land on island, beautiful, people wonderfully friendly. I decide to stay with some others."

Getting Supplies The method of travel for supplies was walking. The climate was warm and the sand hot on bare feet. The supplies bought were fruit, coconuts, fish. The marketplace was open, not really a market. People were trading, and the mood was happy. The money used was pearls, pretty little shells.

Death The date of death was A.D. 1782. The cause was an attack by warriors from the sea. "Fire, blind panic, now only me, fire, home falling around me." He was in "middle age." The feelings after death were: "None, I float back to my cloud."

Life in 1850

The number of cases jumps from 123 in 1700 to 213 in 1850, almost 100 percent increase. Had the population doubled? It had in my sample. The percentage of males to females was very close, 50.5 percent male and 49.5 percent female. The more cases I have in a sample, the closer the ratio I get works out to 50/50. The number of upper class lives went down a little, to 7 percent, in

1850. So many of my subjects were active in colonies in the Americas, South Africa, and other parts of the world that apparently there was little time for the kind of more elaborate lives lived in Europe in 1700. However, the middle class shows an increase. Although they lived simply, many subjects had skills and were not merely farmers plowing the land. Thirty-four percent of them can be classified as artisans, or people with a trade of some kind. Fifty-nine percent of the sample lived lower class lives.

Improvement was to be seen in the areas of longevity and the kinds of deaths experienced. There were fewer accidental and fewer violent deaths than there had been in all the previous time periods. Sixty-four percent of all my subjects died of old age or disease. There were fewer infant deaths than had shown up in my samples in earlier time periods.

The Near East, where so many of my subjects lived such fascinating lives in the B.C. time periods, was represented by only three subjects, or 1 percent of the lives lived in 1850.

Life in Asia was considerably more colorful and civilized in 1850 than it had been in the previous time periods. Twenty of my subjects went to Asia, where most of them now lived in civilized centers, the leather-clad natives of the past being represented by only two regressions among the twenty.

A total of 32 percent of my subjects went to Europe in the 1850s. The lives definitely seemed more civilized now than in earlier time periods, though most of the pageantry and beautiful clothing that was present in the regressions in Europe in the 1700s had disappeared.

The 50 percent, or 106 subjects, who went to lifetimes lived in the United States in 1850 presented a genuine panorama of life in this country during the last century. About two thirds were located in the East and Midwest. There were lives lived in Boston, New York, and Baltimore, but the majority lived in small towns or farms. Many of them moved during this time period; they would start out in one place and wind up further west. Only one third were west of the Mississippi River, and many of these were in the Plains states. Most of my subjects actually came from California, but only five of the 106 lives in the 1800s were reported in California. Several lives were lived as Indians in the 1800s, four were black, and the rest appeared to be Caucasian.

I thought that a number of subjects would go to lives in the Civil War because this era has been so widely depicted in history books, movies, and television—but only three of them seem to have been soldiers during the Civil War. In 1850, only 5 percent of the sample were in South America, and only 3 percent in Africa. Five of the latter lived lives as primitive natives, but the sixth life was that of a British soldier in South Africa.

The next reports provide a final sampling of past lives, these experienced in the 1800s.

TRIP 1

Sex Male as male

Place England, perhaps near Southampton.

Appearance Brown, curly hair, worn in a pigtail. Sometimes wore a white powdered wig.

Dress Shoes were shiny leather with square buckles. Wore knee socks, pants to knees, long waistcoat.

Landscape and Terrain "Bristol Bay, seaport, waterfront, hills surrounding, cobbled narrow streets, clouds moving swiftly, low bright sun beyond." The buildings were three or four storied, with peaked roofs, and were stone or wood framed.

Food and Mealtimes "Meatpie, mashed potatoes?" Squab, mutton. The utensils pictured are a three-tined fork, a knife, and a dull metal plate.

Community Event "On horseback, leading some guards, overtaking an important man in his coach, arresting him (I'm a captain in the 'Service')."

Getting Supplies The money was a coin the size of a half dollar, gold, with a picture of wigged man with long nose. "For God and Country" on coin. Purchased shot and powder and loaded it in wagons. They were returning from scene of battle.

Death Died in 1834 at the age of 34. Shot in chest by horsemen sent "to my home by the man I arrested." Feelings after death: "Happiness, love for all at death scene below me as I leave the body."

TRIP 1

Sex Female as female
Place England
Appearance "Elaborate wig, white, piled high."
Dress Small white slippers. Elaborate dress with blue silk bodice, tight fitting, and white lace skirt. French clothing.
Landscape and Terrain "Green—out in the countryside in a kind of castle or self-contained settlement. Nice day." The only buildings are associated with the castle. "Forest, large green trees. Looks like an English countryside."
Food and Mealtimes "Bread and stew" eaten from hexagonal pewter or silver-colored plates.
Community Event "Country fair."
Getting Supplies Large paper money, buff in color with two circles on it, was used to buy supplies. The supplies were silk cloth. She went to market in a carriage.
Death Death was at age 30 or 40 of consumption. "Died in bed—just sort of wasted away." The feelings after death were: "What a silly, wasted life." She added: "I could not reconcile the fact that I was dressed in seventeenth-century *French* attire but was with people dressed in the attire of the English seventeenth century—a very vivid impression." But the date flashed on at death was 1848.

TRIP 1

Sex Female as female
Place Europe (area not specified).
Appearance "Blond, thick" hair with beautiful long braids. White skin.
Dress "Navy-blue full skirt, white apron, white stockings, lace white cap with points. Wooden clogs."
Landscape and Terrain "Rolling green hills—green, green grass and trees, cool, moist air, sunny day." Small wooden farmhouses were scattered about sparsely.
Food and Mealtimes "Hot thick soup, like an onion borsht," eaten from wooden bowls, using colored wooden spoons with painted flowers on them. The meal was eaten at a long wooden table with ten people. "I was in the middle." It was a "happy family."
Community Event "My sister's wedding. I was wearing white too. Lacy clothes, dancing. Holding hands."

Getting Supplies   Went to market in horse-drawn cart. "I was sitting in back, benches on sides of cart." The coins used had picture of Queen.

Death   Died in 1860 at age 10. "I was ice skating and wouldn't come in when my mother kept calling. I developed pneumonia and died." The feelings about death: "Calmness, sorry to leave family."

TRIP 1

Sex   Female as female

Place   Tulsa, Oklahoma.

Appearance   Blond smooth hair, curly and long.

Dress   Pink-and-white gingham dress of coarse material, fitted bodice, no belt, and several petticoats. The shoes were black Mary Janes with round toes; white stockings. "I am about 18 or 20." Hands are covered with white sheer wrist gloves.

Landscape and Terrain   "Warm, dry, sunny and clear—green rich rolling hills—fertile—some flowers—pond." She saw a whitewashed farm-type house with a large porch in front with a swing.

Food and Mealtimes   Grits with butter, salt and pepper served at a rough table. Ate from a white bowl with blue trim and matching saucer. Used a plain spoon of metal. "Grandfather on right, mother across the table (Sonja)—someone on left but not clear."

Community Event   "Carnival. I was younger (6–8 years)." Wore blue dress and was very happy, excited. "Had a 'flash' of someone drowning in the lake at carnival."

Getting supplies   Went to town in buckboard. "Bought blue fabric with red flowers." It was a country store. "Paid with brown and white currency (U. S. Grant? some numbers) larger than current bills."

Death   Died in 1867 at age 88. "Fell and broke hip and back. No pain, calm. Black dress, white collar, white hair." The feelings about death are "very peaceful as are all others around me." Feelings after death: "Light and airy. Threw kisses to family members. No one was very sad or morbid. It was very 'easy.' "

TRIP 3

Sex   Female as female

Place   Finland or Sweden

Appearance   Very blond hair, shiny, silky in braids. Small hands of a child.

Dress   Brown leather shoes with straps, a dress with a little apron.

Landscape and Terrain   "In a field of rye being harvested. Warm, sunny
   weather."
Community Event   "A christening of a baby or some event with a baby."
Journey   "Made on a wagon pulled by a horse. From a town to my aunt's
   big old house." On the journey saw "a two-story wooden house with
   a wagon wheel out front."
Religious Ceremony   A wedding, at which she wore a white dress and
   was happy. Heard singing.
Death   Died at about age 10 in 1877. The body was marked with sores.
   The cause of death was "a disease, smallpox or something." After death:
   "Didn't want to leave my body, reluctant to die. Felt sorry for my
   grieving mother." The body was buried in a plain wooden box.

Life in the Twentieth Century

Forty-seven, or 4 percent, of my subjects reported lives lived at
least in part in the twentieth century. The social-class figures were
quite comparable to those in 1850, with 6 percent of the subjects
falling into the upper class, 30 percent of them into the middle
class, and 64 percent of them into the lower class. The major difference in the twentieth century is in the cause of death: 47 percent
of the deaths reported in this century were natural, 13 percent
were accidental, and a full 32 percent were reported as violent.
Most of these violent deaths were in World Wars I and II, and I
couldn't help speculating about the possibility that people who died
violently in wars return to new incarnations much more quickly
than subjects who die naturally. This is too small a sample on
which to base a conclusion but it does warrant further research.

Not all deaths in warfare in the 1900s were the result of sophisticated weaponry and bombs. A primitive lifetime was experienced
by a male subject who saw himself as a male on one of the South
Seas Islands. "I have bare feet and I'm standing on a boat with
slats and water beneath. I'm wearing some kind of woven and
patterned tight-fitting garment on the hips. It seems to have a grass
fringe. My hair is black and long and fluffy rather than straight.
I am a man. When you asked about landscape, I saw a mountainous

island with lots of forest and other islands in sight. The community event was a group of men preparing for an invasion of the neighboring island. Our journey was made by boat with long oars. When nearing the island, a village came into sight. We were pounding our spears on the bottom of the boat as a war cry. I was glad to see that our attack was a surprise, and we entered the village unseen. The religious ceremony was preparation for war with men in paint and women watching from the perimeter. The women are naked. The musical sounds were chanting with wooden dowels being struck together. The purpose of the ceremony was to summon protection from the gods; my feeling was excitement, pride, and fear."

12
WHAT DOES IT ALL MEAN?

The graphs and tables in Chapter 8 sum up in numerical terms findings based on thousands of hours spent roaming in other people's right brains. When I look back over those many hours, a montage of impressions stays with me.

I remember the frustrated feeling of the subjects (approximately 10 percent) who either were unable to get any impressions or who went into a deep sleep during the first induction, and only woke up when I brought them back to reality. They would ask me, "Is it because I never had a lifetime before?" I remember laughing and saying I had no idea; but as my workshops progressed, I began to be able to identify more precisely my sleepers and my wide-awakers (those people who didn't seem to get any impression). The latter fell into two groups. One was made up of subjects who believed deeply in reincarnation and were searching for a sudden experience of illumination regarding a past life. It mattered very much to them, and their ego was deeply involved in the whole procedure. The very intensity of their wish is what keeps such subjects from going under hypnosis. They are much like the people who look forward to something important happening the next day and tell themselves they must go to sleep. But the more they tell themselves they have to sleep, the more wide awake they become. Another group of my wide-awakers were people who were very doubtful about reincarnation and whose egos felt intensely uncomfortable at the idea of "letting go." These subjects seemed highly self-critical, and occasionally one of them would tell me, "I *knew* I couldn't do this."

Among my sound-asleepers were people who had done a great deal of meditation or who had learned self-hypnosis. Some of them were hypnotists in their own right. These subjects went into deep trance almost as soon as I took them to the relaxation procedure. It seemed as though they slipped easily into their right brains and, when they were there, went to their own places. The hypnotist's voice became lost, and they drifted into colors and spaces far from the reach of my hypnotic instructions. These subjects almost always came awake just as I was beginning the procedure of bringing the subjects out of hypnosis, indicating that at very deep levels they were indeed aware of my voice.

I also remember the doubts and hesitations of my subjects on the first trip, and their anxiety that they could not be hypnotized. I remember their amazement at the foreshortening of the time under hypnosis. I also remember their reactions to their realization that they were following my instructions even before I spoke them. "It seemed so natural under hypnosis for me to do what you were asking me. Sometimes I felt irritation because you were so slow. I had already done the thing you were asking us about."

The discovery of the telepathic relationship between the hypnotist and the subjects gave me pause. Not only did I have to be careful that I asked the same questions of every group, so that I could evaluate the variation in the responses fairly, but I also had to make sure that they could not pick up bits of information from me about past time periods. I struggled with this concern for some time, and finally decided that if my subjects were giving me data that I expected, I didn't know how they were doing it. The subjects who saw the same types of buildings in the same time periods were hypnotized in different workshops in different places, and long before I had tabulated and evaluated the data. Because I couldn't have known the similarity in their observations at the time of the hypnotic recalls, they couldn't have picked up anything from me telepathically. And certainly they couldn't know which of them were supposed to be male and which female in any regression group in order to align the statistics for, say, the A.D. 1200 time period. Telepathic contact does not involve statistical enumeration, but rather seems to entail the flashing of sensory bits of data and instructions. Therefore, although some people may question my research on the basis of telepathic clues received during the experiments, to me any such cues do not invalidate the overall statistical findings.

One of the intriguing aspects of my subjects' discussions of their experiences was the emergence of little fragments of information about past time periods, such as the strange fact that forks changed number of tines over the centuries. I found my subjects' accurate observations interesting and suggestive, although it is not the kind of conclusive evidence represented by the statistics on population and sex distribution in past lives.

Another area that yielded suggestive but inconclusive data was money, which I had thought would be a very good index for checking past-life recall. I discovered that many different kinds of coins were used in all parts of the world, but it was hard to get descriptions precise enough to provide information for checking. I did learn that there had been an octagonal coin (my subjects described it as squarish, with the corners pounded to make it look more round, and with a hole in the middle) that first appeared in 500 B.C. around the southern rim of the Mediterranean Sea, and was apparently in widespread use through the A.D. 25 period. One such coin popped up in twelfth-century recall. Paper money seems to have been universally used only in the 1800s and after; and even in this time period, coins were more common than paper money. This finding does conform to historical reality, and so does the reporting of great diversity of coins and bills. A modern monetary system such as the one we have today did not come into existence in this country until well after the Civil War. Paper money reported by my subjects in the United States in the nineteenth century did check out accurately in many cases.

I have not done any formal follow-up of the subjects in my groups. Many of them have been in touch with me and told me that the experience of past-life recall was meaningful in their lives. Although I am sure there are others to whom it was no more than a long day spent lying on a floor, I do believe that for the majority, the experience was something they will remember for many years, a door opening. But opening onto what? For some, it was another facet in the long journey of enlightenment about the workings of their inner minds. For others it was a form of entertainment. Each subject is as unique in his or her reactions and inner mind as in his fingerprints.

As discussed in Chapter 8, some subjects reported phobias dissolving as a result of experiencing a death in a past lifetime. Typical comments were:

"I used to be terrified of water, but since I experienced drowning in the past lifetime, I don't seem to fear it anymore."

"I used to be afraid of horses, I never knew why. Now that I know that a horse kicked me and I died back in that lifetime in the 1700s, I understand it better. I'm still not entirely over my fear of horses, but I feel much more comfortable around them."

It may well be that past-life recall for the purpose of overcoming irrational fears will become more and more common in our society. Anything that helps people would seem to be a good idea, even though we may not be able to find a rationale for it in our philosophical concepts. If it works, we are likely to use it.

In addition to the data from my graphs and tables, feedback from some of my subjects who researched their own experiences in my hypnotic workshop has provided another level of evidence. As I have not conducted this research personally, what I am reporting now is essentially hearsay.

A young sailor had experienced a past life in A.D. 800 in an island of the South Pacific. His map showed Indonesia. He was eating a strange kind of nut, one he had never seen before. He reported to me later that he had come across a picture of the nut he was eating in a subsequent issue of the *National Geographic.*

"It looked exactly like what I saw under hypnosis," he said. "The article said that this nut was found only on the island of Bali."

Another subject had seen herself as a knight in a past life in 1200. "I thought to myself that this was really trite and must be a fantasy," she reported to me. "I looked down at my feet and saw a triangular toeplate. I thought to myself that it should be round, like the armor I had seen in museums. I looked it up in an encyclopedia and found the triangular toeplate illustrated. The encyclopedia reported that this triangular toeplate was used only in Italy and only until the year 1280. In the past-life regression, I lived in Italy and died in 1254."

What does my research study prove? The answer is up to each reader. We live in a culture in which myths are colliding, and new concepts jostling one another in a ferment of change. What exactly is man? The following grab bag of myths offer the answers. Help yourself, or better yet, make your own synthesis.

Myth A. The myth of the hard-nosed scientist.

The hard-nosed scientist knows full well there is only one reality, and it lies outside his skin. This reality is seen as being serious, difficult, real, and the only thing worth paying attention to. Any of the inner functions of the mind are regarded by the hard-nosed scientist as imagination, subjective in nature and outside of his field of interest. According to this myth, consciousness is an accidental byproduct of the evolution of brain cells. Our gray matter, our cortex, produces consciousness in the same way that the heart pumps blood. Mind has a function, but it is only to relate man to his environment and what happens in it. Internal events are left to such creatures as poets, musicians, women, primitive peoples.

The hard-nosed scientist myth requires that all instances of subjective experiencing be relegated to a realm called fantasy. Fantasy, by definition, is accidental and coincidental, and therefore, by implication, trivial; it can have no real interest to a serious-minded person. The results of my study, as viewed by the hard-nosed scientist, are no more than a curiosity. He would claim that people say these things under hypnosis because they're influenced by the hypnotist and they like to make up interesting, imaginative stories, much like five-year-olds. The entire subject is of no consequence, in terms of the myth of the hard-nosed scientist.

Myth B. The Maximum Leader, or the I-will-show-you-heaven myth.

This is a very popular myth. If we adhere to this myth, we know that we are alive and that the world is real, but we also feel that there is a boss over all of us, as there is in our regular tribal and everyday life. This boss is someone who created the world and therefore has complete control over it and over us. We cannot know or understand the boss-of-it-all, to whom we give the name God, but now and then there are certain very smart people who are given a special channel through which they can communicate with this Boss of the Universe.

According to this myth, the smart person who can communicate with the Boss of the Universe then spreads his messages through those who become Believers. The notion of being a channel for a pure Godlike spirit is the distinguishing quality of the intermediary between God and man. This myth has many variations—as many variations as the people who are designated appropriate channels from the Boss of the Universe to you and me. They could be Joseph Smith, Moses, Buddha, Mohammed, Jesus, and a host of others. The nature of the messages channeled through the intermediary, whom we call the religious leader, tends to be essentially unvarying, even though they are colored by the social environment in which the interpreter lives.

What happens with this myth is that the accumulated superstitions that accompany every "revelation" begin to take on more prominence than the essential message, which is one of love and one-ness with the universe. Then human beings argue over which divine leader has the best channel to the Boss of the Universe, and the arguments lead to everything from religious wars to splits in church groups over which dogma is correct. The essential thrust of a Myth B belief system is that you and I are humble and inadequate servants of a distant Boss of the Universe whose mysterious ways can only be interpreted through an essentially pure spirit. If this spirit doesn't preach reincarnation, then reincarnation doesn't exist.

Myth C. The reincarnation myth as the West interprets it from Eastern religious sources.

In Myth C, the notion of the Boss of the Universe is retained, but the emphasis is placed upon the procedure through which souls progress to reunion with the Boss of the Universe. This belief system involves the notion that one starts out as a spark of the Universal Light, becoming a new soul and incarnating in earth, and then following a slow and laborious pathway through many different lifetimes from young soul to old soul. The young soul enters the body eagerly but makes many mistakes. The more mistakes he makes, the more lives he has to live laboriously, until he finally erases all his karma. Toward the end of his upward progression through time, he begins a series of lives in which he starts on the spiritual path. He finally reaches that last lifetime, in which he is able to transcend the physical universe. At this point he gets to be part of the Great White Light, which is another term for God. Some individual souls who have progressed to the point of becoming part of God are willing to return to earth to help other seekers along the arduous path through time and through various bodies and lifetimes. These are the avatars or helpers, who have erased all their karma, but are returning to enlighten the rest of us.

Myth D. The quantum physicist myth.

The quantum physicist is a scientist who doesn't entirely agree with the hard-nosed scientist, because his researches have taken him into new realms. The physicist understands Einstein's equation $E=mc^2$, and realizes that there is no material world unless energy happens to be moving at a speed we can comprehend (the speed of light). His new tools have revealed to him the nature of the building blocks of matter, which turn out to be not building blocks at all, but quantum flows of energy moving in waves. These little bits of energy seem to have free will, and appear and disappear in material reality depending on their speed and other factors.

Therefore, the physicist understands that the real world is not real. In this sense, he agrees with the Indian mystics who state that we live in a "veil of maya," or illusion. Quantum physicists like to play on the outer fringes of the universe and the outer fringes of concept creation. They relish black holes and anti-matter, and fiddle with new machines that help reveal to us the strange nature of the laws governing energy outside of our usual physical framework. The quantum physicist is more interested in the new developments in mind-brain studies than is the biological scientist. The biological scientist is still tinkering with the physical body and the physical mind in an attempt to control our evolution. He is wedded to the notion of space and the notion of time, and operates within that framework. The quantum physicist understands that the framework of space and time melt around the edges and merge into other universes.

Myth E. Seth.

Jane Roberts, a writer in Elmira, New York, has become a trance medium. The entity that speaks through Jane is called Seth. Seth has a very interesting myth. In essence, Seth carries the insights of the quantum physicist into wider dimensions and suggests some of the laws governing energy that is operating outside of time and space.

This myth proposes that the emotions generated by consciousness are the motive power of the physical universe. Emotions generate waves of direct energy. A directed emotion operates on a subatomic particle, which Seth calls the EUG, or monopole—a tiny bit of energy with one magnetic pole and a magnetic field. Emotion pulls together the monopoles, which in turn form electrons, neutrons, and so on down the line. Thus, the world of physical reality is built up from the emotional energy generated by consciousness. In this sense, consciousness is seen as creating bodies, lifetimes, and historical eras. Time does not exist for consciousness; it is one of the creations of consciousness, almost like the stage a carpenter constructs on which a play can take place. In the same way, consciousness uses the monopole to create the atoms and molecules of our body, generating a costume that we wear in order to enact the play we call being alive in any given historical era.

Myth F. The Wambach myth, or, Do it yourself!

As the author of this book, I get first crack at making my own myth. I heartily recommend to the reader that he construct his or her own too.

Basically the Wambach myth says that reincarnation is a handy concept, and it does take our notions of ourselves farther than the more humble approaches of Myth A and Myth B. I feel all of us are like apple trees. We have trunks and roots, limbs and leaves, and we also produce apples. The apples we produce are individual egos and life experiences. Each apple on the tree has within itself all the essence of the entire tree. In this way, the DNA molecules in the seeds of the apples are the tiny sparks of God in all of us. When people are hypnotized and sent back to a past life, the apples—instead of looking outside of their little green skins at the passing caterpillar, the sunshine and rain—are directed back into their stems, up through the limbs to the trunk of the tree. It is this trunk of the tree that I call the superconsciousness.

When I hypnotize people, I think that what I do is take them through the trunk to the opposite side of the tree and out to a branch, where I say, "There's another apple; look through that skin and see what the sunshine looks like over there, what's the caterpillar situation, and do you feel a breeze blowing?" In that sense, there are many lives we can all experience in the tree, which is our entity self. The tree can know the experience of each of the apples that is growing at any given season.

This myth gets a little complicated, because apple trees also have cycles. Apple trees are born, live, and die just as do the individual apples they bear. I believe that we go through a process of having lives just as an apple tree goes through the process of fruiting and flowering and producing many seasons of apples before it finally takes leave of physical reality. In a sense, then, our entities have a life span within physical reality, but within that lifetime have many different apples, or lives. When an entity has produced enough in physical reality, it leaves behind during its last season apples that contain the seeds of its own entity self. These are apples that sprout, and one of them may grow into another apple tree in the same location. Thus, consciousness moves ever onward, creating and creating; and all the experiences of all the apple trees before the apple tree entity you are now are available to you through your right-brain tuner.

The basic question in this last half of the twentieth century is whether mind is primary and matter a result of mind or consciousness, as opposed to the older idea in our culture that mind is an accidental creation of evolution and the development of the nervous system. Like most such arguments in the past history of ideas, it is likely that it will be resolved by the elaboration of a concept capable of combining both in a new unified system of thought.